D1306723

Rudyard Kipling's India

Rudyard Kipling's India

By K. Bhaskara Rao, 1926 —

The Emmet O'Neal Library
Mountain Brook, Alabama

University of Oklahoma Press : Norman

R 828x
Kipling

By K. Bhaskara Rao

Yachts, Hamburgers, and a Hindu (Bangalore, 1962)
Candle Against the Wind (Bangalore, 1963)
Rudyard Kipling's India (Norman, 1967)

The paper on which this book is printed bears the watermark of the University of Oklahoma Press and is designed for an effective life of at least three hundred years.

Library of Congress Catalog Card Number: 67–10208

Copyright 1967 by the University of Oklahoma Press, Publishing Division of the University. Composed and printed at Norman, Oklahoma, U.S.A., by the University of Oklahoma Press. First edition.

To My Father

461 4.95 11-3-78

c.1

Acknowledgments

I WISH TO EXPRESS my deep gratitude to these members of the faculty in the State University of Iowa: To Professor William R. Irwin, for his encouragement, patience, and valuable criticism, and to Professor Frederick P. W. McDowell, for suggesting the topic of this study and guiding it during its earlier stages.

K. BHASKARA RAO

San Francisco, California
November 10, 1966

Contents

Rudyard Kipling's India

Kipling's Place as a Writer on India: the Necessity for a New Evaluation

WE ARE TOO CLOSE to the events to evaluate with objectivity the British impact on India. With the attainment of Indian independence in 1947, British imperialism suffered a severe setback. We must, however, remember, as Sir Percival Griffiths points out, that since imperialism has been one of the most important channels by which civilization has been diffused, it cannot be condemned in itself, but must be judged by its results.[1] Imperial Rome conferred great benefits on mankind, particularly in the realm of law and public administration, while the Norman conquest of England provided the impulse which was in the course of time to stimulate nationalism and the unique political genius of the English national character. In India itself, the full-blooded imperialism of the Guptas during the sixth century B.C. carried the culture of India in the form of art, music, and Sanskrit literature to southern Asia.[2]

The British conquest and administration of India, lasting for more than 150 years, linked India with the technological attainments and political ideologies of the Western World. Ambitious irrigation projects were launched. Canals and dams, railways and telegraph lines drew together the different parts of the country. Politically—partly by deliberate act, partly by exposure to the new influences of the modern world—the British in India promoted parliamentary constitutional, and cabinet government.

There is, however, another side to this picture, that of the evils

[1] *The British Impact on India*, 15.
[2] *Ibid.*

3

of colonialism resulting in material exploitation of the natives and moral degeneration of the imperial masters. Such a picture has been masterfully presented by George Orwell in his novel *Burmese Days*. Flory, the self-critical Englishman, questions the "usefulness" of British rule:

> "Bosh, my dear Doctor. We teach young men to drink whisky and play football, I admit, but precious little else. Look at our schools—factories for cheap clerks. We've never taught a single useful manual trade to the Indians. We've even crushed various industries. Where are the Indian muslins now? Back in the forties or thereabouts they were building sea-going ships in India, and manning them as well. Now you couldn't build a seaworthy fishing boat there. In the eighteenth century the Indians cast guns that were at any rate up to the European standard. Now after we've been in India a hundred and fifty years, you can't make so much as a brass cartridge case in the whole continent. The only Eastern races that have developed at all are the independent ones. I won't instance Japan, but take the case of Siam."[3]

Orwell thus appears to contend that British imperialism in its philosophical concept was not based upon the humanistic idea of offering assistance to the underprivileged, but rather emerged from England's assumed moral responsibility for governing an alien people. He is highly critical of such an attitude; it was, he believes, detrimental to good human relationships. It resulted in what E. M. Forster termed "the undeveloped heart" on the part of the rulers, thereby creating a sharp cleavage between the alien ruler and the native. The Indian became a stranger in his own land. The idea of belonging to a subject, and therefore inferior, race hindered his moral and mental development. He lost initiative, lacked determination, and slavishly imitated his masters. Being a poor and indiscriminate imitator, he became the butt of all ridicule.

It is against this complex interpretation of British rule in India, its achievement and its failure, that one must study Rudyard Kipling, a writer whose mind and spirit were dedicated to the glorification of the British Empire and the Anglo-Saxon race.

[3] *Burmese Days,* 249.

4

For Kipling, literature and politics were interactive, and without this fusion he would not have emerged as a successful writer. His youth coincided with England's period of glorious expansion. He thrilled to the exploits of the British Army as they brought distant lands and strange peoples under the British crown. Had he been physically able, he might have enlisted as a soldier fighting for the Queen in "Afghan snows." But we know that he suffered from poor eyesight. Physically handicapped, Kipling yearned to serve his Queen and his country, and writing provided the outlet for his loyal emotions.

While it is true that politicians and statesmen like Disraeli, Gladstone, Sir John Seeley, and Joseph Chamberlain were responsible for British imperialism, it was in reality a movement with widely diffused emotional sources, as D. C. Somervell indicates:

> For the Imperialism of the late Victorian period went deeper than any political action or political theory. Its greatest exponent was not Sir John Seeley, nor even Joseph Chamberlain, most notable of Colonial Secretaries. Imperialism was a sentiment rather than a policy; its foundations were moral rather than intellectual; its greatest exponent was Rudyard Kipling.[4]

Calling upon the English people to consider the Empire as a sacred trust, Kipling made a religion out of the imperial theme. He laid stress on the superiority of the Anglo-Saxon race. He invested it with a new power and position by expounding the doctrine of the "white man's burden." All his Indian writings can be considered an amplification and interpretation of this doctrine.

Kipling was, during his time, not only a forceful writer but also a vital historic force. As a journalist in India he wrote no powerful editorials or articles to influence British government policy in Simla or Delhi; but the tales he casually wrote to fill up the vacant columns of the *Civil and Military Gazette* had a great impact upon English public opinion toward India during the latter part of the nineteenth century. To the average Englishman, Kipling expressed for the first time his own chauvinistic sentiments and ideas in a firm, clear, and colloquial manner. Kipling's stern but simple phi-

[4] *English Thought in the Nineteenth Century,* 186.

5

losophy of action was appealing because he communicated his message in a speech that was as native to the English soil as the rose or the oak. That Kipling was born in India added greater force and authenticity to what he had to say. He soon built up a reputation, therefore, for possessing an insight into native Indian character and life. Moreover, he assumed the role of a prophet when he wrote the "Recessional" and made use of an Old Testament philosophy of history, describing the English as the chosen people of God for service in His cause. Beginning as a casual journalist on an Indian newspaper, Kipling became a prophetic force.

With his potentialities for artistic expression and a responsive audience Kipling could have interpreted Indian life in a way that would have increased good feeling between the English and the Indians. Unfortunately, his interpretation was not without bias, with the result that it created ill feeling between the two communities. Aware of the extent of Kipling's real influence Gilbert Murray stated in his inaugural address before the Conference of Nationalities and Subject Races held in London in 1910:

> If ever it were my fate to put men in prison for the books they write, I should not like it, but I should know where to begin. I should first of all look up my old friend, Rudyard Kipling, because in several stories he has used his great powers to stir up in the minds of hundreds of thousands of Englishmen a blind and savage contempt for the Bengali. And many Bengalis naturally have read these stories. You cannot cherish a savage contempt for anyone without its being quickly reciprocated. And when both sides regard each other with the same savage contempt, it is not likely that they can dwell together in peace.[5]

Such prejudices towards a nation and its people were possible because Kipling looked at India from the perspective of a self-assumed superiority. To be ruled by Britain was India's obligation; to rule India was Britain's duty. This was the rigid opinion of Kipling. Many of the conservative imperialists of the latter part of the nineteenth century also held such a view; but imperialism

[5] Jabez T. Sunderland, *India in Bondage: Her Right to Freedom and a Place Among the Great Nations*, 103.

6

itself progressed from the conservatism of Sir John Seeley, who believed in colonizing a country as an end in itself, to the liberalism of Gladstone, who believed that the object of colonization was to create "so many happy Englands."[6] King George V advocated preparing India for eventual self-government within the framework of the British Commonwealth. She was to be granted dominion status, but not that of a republic. Although both India and the men around him were changing, Kipling remained in a static frame of mind. To explain Rudyard Kipling, therefore, is to explain the earlier phase of British imperialism in India.

In published assessments of Kipling's life and writings, no exhaustive and authoritative study of his treatment of India is to be found. Hilton Brown, in his book *Rudyard Kipling* (1945), devotes a chapter entitled "Kuppleen Sahib" to a discussion of Kipling's understanding of India. Brown, who spent some time in India and wrote a novel, *Torteval*, concerning Indian life, makes no claim to any special research and pays but casual attention to Kipling's Indian writings in his brief discussion. His book accordingly does not constitute a serious study of Kipling's India.

The Indians read Kipling extensively but evinced no critical interest in his writings, obviously because of his unceasing championship of racial superiority, opposition to Indian freedom, and ridicule of the educated Indian, which stereotyped his views as lacking depth of understanding and intellectual keenness. But an Indian point of view is essential to an evaluation of Kipling's fidelity to the Indian scene.

There are in existence brief discussions of Kipling by four Indian writers. A. R. Sarath-Roy, in an article for the *North American Review*, "Rudyard Kipling Through Hindu Eyes," considers Kipling to be a British propagandist engaged in slighting the Indian character, with no understanding of India.[7] Roy is emotionally involved and loses his critical perspective. One can understand his sentiments in view of the fact that Roy is a Bengali and Kipling

---

[6] W. E. Gladstone, *Kin Beyond the Sea* (Boston, 1868), 12.

[7] "Rudyard Kipling Through Hindu Eyes," *North American Review*, Vol. CXCIX (February, 1914), 274.

was particularly prejudiced against the Bengali. A second article published in the *Calcutta Review* by M. M. Bhattacharjee, also a Bengali, is a general survey of Kipling's writings, with emphasis on his skill in the art of constructing the short story.[8] It makes no attempt to relate Kipling's stories to the actualities of Indian life. The next is a brief essay in *Lippincott's Magazine* by "An Indian Student," in which the writer credits Kipling with the capacity to describe Indian scenes superficially, but criticizes him for lacking an insight into Indian life.[9] Bhupal Singh, in *A Study of Anglo-Indian Fiction*, discusses Kipling's influence on other Anglo-Indian writers.[10] All of these discussions are journalistic rather than scholarly and come to the expected conclusion that Kipling could not understand India. It is Kipling's belief in racial superiority that the authors censure, on the grounds that such a belief always considers the colonial an inferior being. None of these Indian writers analyze *Kim*, Kipling's greatest work, in which he came closest to understanding India. It was in *Kim*, as we shall see later, that Kipling sensed the fundamental unity of India amidst its diversity. Furthermore, all these accounts of Kipling were written prior to Indian independence, and thus reflect an attitude particularly hostile to him. Hence another look at Kipling's India is necessary.

I propose, therefore, to evaluate Rudyard Kipling's treatment of India in his short stories, his poems, and his two novels, *Kim* and *Naulahka*.

India had exerted a great fascination over the minds of English authors long before Kipling started to write. This interest was a result of the tales that sailors and traders brought back to England after voyaging on the new sea route to India. The subcontinent came to be associated with exotic adventure and fabulous wealth. Earlier English writers, including Marlowe, Shakespeare, and Milton, conjured up a vision of India as a land of untold wealth, of barbaric pearls and gold.

[8] "Rudyard Kipling," *Calcutta Review*, Vol. LIX (April–May, 1936), 97–106, 177–89.
[9] "Kipling's Conception of India," *Lippincott's Monthly Magazine*, Vol. XCIV (August, 1914), 177.
[10] *A Survey of Anglo-Indian Fiction* (London, 1934), 68–74.

It was these tales of wealth that stimulated the founding of the East India Company in 1601. Permanently established in India in 1702, the operations of the company led to more concrete interest in and more detailed knowledge of India. The shareholders of the company were rewarded with generous dividends, thereby bringing increased prosperity to Englishmen at home at the expense of Indians exploited by company men. Samuel Foote, the eighteenth-century dramatist, in his play *The Nabob*, exposes in the character of Sir Matthew Mite, the type of unscrupulous Anglo-Indian company man who, "from small beginnings and obscure origins, had raised immense fortunes in a very short period" at the cost of impoverishing the natives.[11] In David Garrick's play *The Clandestine Marriage*, we find references to the rise and fall of East India Company shares and the consequent effect upon everyday life in England. Edmund Burke's description of the company's servants is no exaggeration:

> Animated with all the avarice of age, and all the impetuosity of youth, they roll in one after another; wave after wave; and there is nothing before the eyes of the natives but an endless, hopeless prospect of new flights of birds of prey and passage, with appetites continually renewing for a food that is continually wasting.[12]

Burke was one of the very few who realized the importance of India to Englishmen. He spoke of England's duty to rule India with justice and understanding, but his attitude was free from any racial superiority.

With Clive's victories in Bengal, the foundations for British empire in India were firmly laid, and the latter part of the eighteenth century witnessed an increasing number of Englishmen in India. Coming to a strange land, the Englishmen in India sought for companionship among themselves. They lived together in groups and separate colonies, thereby forming a distinctive, isolated community which came to be called the Anglo-Indian community. They wrote about their new experiences, their devotion to England, and their hardships in adjusting to the new situations. These

[11] *The Memoirs of Samuel Foote*, ed. by William Cook, I, 175.
[12] "Speech on Mr. Fox's East India Bill," *Works*, II, 462.

writings constitute Anglo-Indian literature, which during two centuries has had many contributors, of whom the three most important are Rudyard Kipling, E. M. Forster, and John Masters. Each, as will be seen, represents an important and different phase in Anglo-Indian writing.

Kipling looked at the Indian problem as part of the white man's burden. Hence he tried to justify England's attempts to hold and tame "the new caught sullen people." Britain was in India, according to Kipling, for India's own good. He therefore presented the sufferings of his countrymen in governing India, while he completely and conveniently forgot the hardships and humiliations that the Indians suffered at the hands of the British. Thus Kipling represents the condescending attitude of the staunch imperialist toward the Indian people. Forster's *A Passage to India* can be considered a corrective to Kipling in that it presents forcefully the humiliations suffered by the Indians under British officials. Forster was writing in a new political and intellectual climate of English liberalism, which opposed the aggressive imperialism of Joseph Chamberlain and critically examined the necessity for the existence of the British empire.

While Kipling's writings served to point out the necessity for the British to remain in India, Forster's single novel proved to be an important document in influencing British departure from India. Nirad C. Chaudhuri pointed out this fact in his review of the novel:

> *A Passage to India* became a powerful weapon in the hands of the anti-imperialists, and was made to contribute its share to the disappearance of British rule in India.[13]

In *A Passage to India*, Forster lays bare the Anglo-Indian problem, which he sees as the result of "an undeveloped heart" on the part of the British. Thus he calls for better interpersonal relationships, making a human appeal to a political case. A more detailed examination of this novel will be made while discussing Kipling's works. Suffice it here to note that Forster represents the liberal, the more tolerant and understanding approach to India.

[13] "Passage to and from India," *Encounter*, Vol. II (June, 1954), 19.

John Masters is a writer on India after independence. He was born in Calcutta in 1914, a member of the fifth generation of his family to serve India, spending fourteen years with the Fourth Gurkha Regiment, a unit of the Indian Army. Masters' book *Bugles and a Tiger* (1956), "A Volume of Autobiography" as he calls it, records in minute detail these rugged years of outdoor army experiences. For most of the time the unit was in the North Western Frontier Provinces, and Masters evokes the active life of these regions with a sureness of touch and incisive realism. The portrait of the courageous Gurkha, the short, stocky Nepali Hindu with mongoloid features who comes closest to Masters' concept of a perfect soldier, is presented with deep understanding and admiration. It is because of this intensive human study of the Gurkha that *Bugles and a Tiger* is valuable.

Masters' knowledge of army life on the Indian frontier gives a true note of authenticity. This area is his main forte. But when he steps outside it to represent the social and political aspects of India, his writings assume a wild and exotic atmosphere with very little basis in reality. Take, for example, *Coromandel!* (1955), the first novel in a series of thirty-five that Masters proposes to write about India, covering the history of Anglo-Indian relations from 1600 to 1947 as reflected in the activities of the Savages, an English family. *Coromandel!* is concerned with the coming of the first Englishman, Jason Savage, to India. Savage's journey is prompted by a treasure map found in England. As generally happens on treasure hunts, he meets with a number of strange adventures, including a romantic episode with an Indian prostitute. There is a conscious attempt on Masters' part to produce an impression of India as a quaint, mysterious, wondrous land. In making such an attempt, he has removed himself far from reality, and since his series of novels purports to be an account of the British in India, a basic fidelity to the Indian scene is essential. *Coromandel!* was aptly described in the *New York Times Book Review* as "wildly implausible escape fiction."[14]

[14] John Barkham, Review of *Coromandel!*, *New York Times Book Review,* March 24, 1954, p. 12.

Bhowani Junction, another novel in John Masters' ambitiously projected series, is set in the year 1946, India on the eve of British departure. Here Masters purports to present the racial problem of the Eurasian. The Eurasian, or Anglo-Indian as he was also called, looked to the British for inspiration. He called England "home" and imitated English manners and customs. As a result, he was opposed to any national movement by Indians and looked down upon them, forgetting that he himself had Indian blood. When the British were about to leave, the Anglo-Indian faced the dilemma of whether to stay in independent India and accept it as "home" or go to England, which he had not seen but had been calling "home." The British did not want him, since he would pose a new racial problem in England. Furthermore, England already faced the problem of providing suitable employment for Englishmen returning from India, and the influx of four million Anglo-Indians would only make matters worse. Many of the Anglo-Indians stayed in India, where they were accepted as full-fledged citizens.

In *Bhowani Junction*, Masters tries to reveal the complex emotions that possessed these Anglo-Indians on the eve of independence. He could have made a penetrating study of a community seeking a new set of values. The character of Victoria Jones, an Anglo-Indian who attempts to identify herself with the new feeling of becoming an "Indian," has great possibilities. But Masters abandons the social problem to concentrate on train wrecks, murders, Communist conspiracies, and the foolishness of the Congress party. He becomes sensationalistic, thereby making *Bhowani Junction* an exotic tale of rape, murder, and violence in India. A perceptive reader can only agree with Lewis Gannett's review of the book in the *New York Herald-Tribune*: "Despite its brilliant flashes of color and its touches of condescending sympathy, *Bhowani Junction* seems out of date in A.D. 1954."[15]

In the course of his autobiography, *Bugles and a Tiger*, Masters satirizes "Hollywoodish conceptions of India" and professes his views on India to be sensible:

[15] Review of *Bhowani Junction*, *New York Herald Tribune Book Review*, March 28, 1954, p. 11.

I had never had the attitude of the average civilian tourist, so I did not think of India as quaint, picturesque, exploited, inscrutable, or other worldly. I thought India was ugly, beautiful, smelly, predictable, and as material as the West. It was inhabited not by yogis and saints, but by people—knaves, giants, dwarfs, and plain people—of various shades of brown.[16]

In spite of this emphasis on his attempt to be realistic, *Coromandel! Bhowani Junction,* and *The Night Runners of Bengal* (based on the Indian Mutiny of 1857) seem particularly suited to Hollywood productions of India, "grand, mysterious, bloody, violent and brutally barbaric."

Masters is in many respects the direct literary descendant of Rudyard Kipling. That he admires Kipling is evident. *Bugles and a Tiger* contains a profusion of complimentary references to Kipling's writings. Masters possesses the same powers of observation and scenic description and a sensuous awareness of the sounds and smells and colors of India. He shares, as Lewis Gannett pointed out in a review of *Bhowani Junction,* Kipling's belief in the white man's burden, the civilizing mission of the Anglo-Saxon race.[17] The following passage from *Bugles and a Tiger* reveals something of this ideal:

> In whatever spirit the tilling, the land was irrigated with English blood. We were none of us quite strangers, nor ever would be. Nor were we at home, as in our homes. If we loved and served, we were the heralds of some truer service yet to come in the world, running our blind courses in the darkness of our time and throwing a little light in a few places. We were intruders, yet there are illogical necessities in history, which India understands, because India sees no truth in logic. We were imperialists, and perhaps it was for empire that my Uncle Dandy died at Festubert and the Sikhs died across his feet; but the word of their bodies as they lay in the pattern of death was not "lead" or "obey," but "give."[18]

[16] *Bugles and a Tiger,* 75.

[17] Review of *Bhowani Junction, New York Herald Tribune Book Review,* March 28, 1954.

[18] Masters, *Bugles and a Tiger,* 299.

The whole passage evokes an image of the Englishman as a man who went out to India only to dedicate his life for the empire. His heroic virtues were part of the Anglo-Saxon myth, which Kipling used and Masters has continued.

There are more specific issues for comparison and contrast between Masters and Kipling, which will be examined in detail later.

It is my intention in the following pages to present Rudyard Kipling's India through consideration of significant factors which influenced him and through careful analysis of his written works.

II

The Lay of the Land: a Boy's Vision

"Ship me somewhere east of Suez,
where the best is like the worst, . . ."
—"MANDALAY."

THE EARL (Marquess) of Dalhousie left India in 1855 with personal satisfaction that British power in India had been firmly established throughout the country. The frontiers on the north and west had been extended to the mountains and on the east to the Bay of Bengal. The native states owed allegiance to and were directed by Britain. The fighting group of Sikhs and Gurkhas and Pathans had been successfully recruited to the imperial forces. There was an increase in revenue as a result of improved methods of land taxation and police administration. Thus when the Earl's successor, Lord Canning, arrived in India in February, 1856, he found the country tranquil enough to give him confidence about the stability of the British empire. Unfortunately his hopes were misplaced, for in the very next year the Indian Mutiny challenged British power in India.

The 1857 Indian uprising was not an organized nationalistic movement; yet it was a demonstration of Indian unrest and resulted in violence on both sides. Memories of the Cawnpore massacre considerably changed the picture of romantic, mystic India that many Englishmen had acquired from reading books like the *Arabian Nights*, which had helped to establish the popular conception of the East. As a result of widespread interest and indignation, the Mutiny of 1857 became a theme for Anglo-Indian writers. Nearly forty years later a writer in *Blackwood's Magazine* again expressed the fond hope that Kipling would make use of the Mutiny for his "magnum opus":

> When Mr. Rudyard Kipling's "magnum opus" appears, may it deal with the Mutiny, and may we be there to read it. He knows his India, he knows his British army, and perhaps a greater achievement than either, he knows his Anglo-India in his habit as he lives. Nor is this all, for no sort or condition of men is alien to him, and he can see the good points in good people—a much more difficult matter than seeing those of bad people. He can appreciate John Lawrence as well as John Nicholson, and sympathise—as who that remembers the description of the Highlanders calling upon their God in the watches of the night will deny—with Havelock and his saints as well as with Hodson of Hodson's horse.[1]

Kipling, however, wrote nothing about the Mutiny. In India he was primarily a journalist, confining himself mostly to observing and writing about the immediate world around him, the *"Here and the Now."*[2] Kipling was too far away from the events that had taken place, having been born eight years after the Mutiny. His writing career started about thirty years after the event, and he had little desire, at the time, to direct his imagination toward the recent past.

The Mutiny is in many respects a landmark of great importance in the history of Anglo-Indian relations. After the suppression of the revolt, the control of India passed from the East India Company to the Crown. Queen Victoria's royal proclamation at this time contained a declaration that all British subjects, including Indians, were to be treated equally. Clemency was to be granted to all offenders not directly involved in the murder of British subjects. In spite of these efforts to foster a policy of amity between the Indians and the Anglo-Indians, mutual fear and distrust between the two communities persisted. It is true that even before the

[1] "The Indian Mutiny in Fiction," *Blackwood's Magazine*, Vol. CLXI (February, 1897), 231.
[2] Walter Morris Hart, *Kipling the Story Writer*, 6.

Mutiny there existed a feeling of hostility between the native Indian and the Anglo-Indian community, but after the Mutiny the cleavage became sharper and more pronounced. Writing of this enmity, Dennis Kincaid declared in *British Social Life in India, 1608–1937:*

> The effect of the Mutiny on Anglo-India can hardly be exaggerated. It is difficult to see why such terrible bitterness should have been aroused among the English at the first news of revolt. The war was to some extent a civil war and as such inevitably bitter. But this does not explain the strange outburst of racial hatred among the civilian population of Calcutta.[3]

The gross violence displayed by both sides in the Mutiny later shocked sensitive Englishmen and Indians alike. Some Indian intellectuals who felt the need for social and religious reform started constructive national movements of a more peaceful, less revolutionary, nature. The Brahma Samaj, the Arya Samaj, the Prarthana Samaj, and the Rama Krishna Mission were some of the movements dedicated to the reform of Indian religious and social life. Raja Ram Mohan Roy, the founder of the Brahma Samaj, had absorbed the best of Eastern and Western culture, and by his writings and oratory gave great impetus to an Indian intellectual awakening during the latter part of the nineteenth century. He reminds one of Matthew Arnold both in denouncing the Philistinism of his own nation and in trying to eliminate dogma and superstition from the Hindu faith in the hope of fostering a more vital religion. The Brahma Samaj, which he headed, had a nation-wide program. Before the end of 1865 there were fifty-four branches of the society, fifty in Bengal, two in the northwestern provinces and one each in the Punjab and Madras.[4] The Rama Krishna Mission sought to interpret the East to the West and to co-ordinate Hindu religion and Indian society. The Prarthana Samaj devoted itself to social reform, particularly in the breaking up of caste restrictions and improving the status of women and the "Untouchables."

[3] *British Social Life in India: 1608–1937*, 193.
[4] Ramesh C. Mazumdar and Others, *An Advanced History of India*, III, 878.

All these activities were part of the great social, religious, and intellectual awakening that India witnessed during the latter part of the nineteenth century. The violence of the Mutiny was an unfortunate interlude. Rabindranath Tagore has vividly recaptured the energetic intellectual curiosity of the educated Indians of this period in his novel *Gora*, which is set in the years immediately following the Mutiny. It was during this period, called by most Indian historians "The Dawn of New India,"[5] that the Kiplings landed in Bombay in 1865.

The Kipling family had many distinguished members and notable connections. Kipling's great-grandfather on his mother's side had received an invitation to preach directly from John Wesley, and his grandfather had also been a notable Wesleyan preacher. Kipling's three uncles were distinguished men: Sir Edward Burne-Jones, the famous Pre-Raphaelite painter at whose house Kipling came to know such eminent people as Christina Rossetti, Robert Browning, Swinburne, and William Morris, (whom he heard declaim *The Saga of the Burnt Njal*),[6] along with Edward Poynter, another painter, who was influential in securing John Lockwood Kipling's assignment to Lahore; and Alfred Baldwin, the railroad owner whose son, Stanley Baldwin, was Kipling's favorite cousin.

John Lockwood Kipling, Rudyard's father, was a sculptor who had studied at South Kensington and had worked for some time as a potter and designer at Wedgwood's in Burslem. His first Indian appointment was as architectural sculptor in the Bombay School of Fine Arts. He was also the Bombay correspondent of the *Pioneer* of Allahabad. His next assignment was in 1880, when he went to Lahore to assume his new duties as principal of the Mayo School of Art and curator of the Central Museum. In 1891 he published a book, *Beast and Man in India*, with the help of A. P. Watt, Rudyard Kipling's literary agent. This book is important to Kipling critics because it contains several extracts from his newspaper reports to the *Civil and Military Gazette*. The work itself proved a source book for the later *Jungle Books*, and several stories, including

[5] *Ibid.*, 812.
[6] Rudyard Kipling, *Something of Myself*, 16.

"The Mark of the Beast," "The Finances of the Gods," and "Moti Guj, Mutineer," parallel episodes in *Beast and Man in India.*

Typically, the book reveals the condescending attitude of many Englishmen toward things Oriental and Indian. It contains many sweeping generalizations about Indian art and religion and shows a failure to understand the animal myths and symbolism inherent in Indian religious thought. Consider the following comment on Indian historians:

> There are many lies in history, but Hindu writers are remarkable for having deliberately and of set principle ignored all the facts of life. All is done, however, with such an air of conviction and pious purpose that we must use Dr. Johnson's kindly discrimination and say they are not inexcusable, but consecrated liars.[7]

This statement is a classic example of sweeping generalization. The sources of Indian history are both legendary and documentary. The Indian historian had to reconstruct the early phases of Indian history from the early Hindu scriptures, *The Vedas,* and from the two great Indian epics, *The Mahabharatha* and the *Ramayana.* To this extent there is reliance upon legends, but certainly there is no deliberate attempt by Indian historians to ignore the facts.

A similar bold and false statement is made about the training of animals:

> No, the Oriental is not a first rate animal trainer. With almost boundless patience, he has no steadfastness of aim, nor has he sufficient firmness of hand and will to secure confidence and obedience.[8]

While John Lockwood Kipling does not credit the Oriental with the ability to train animals, Rudyard Kipling seems to think otherwise. In his story "Moti Guj, Mutineer," we find the splendid example of a native Indian controlling and securing the confidence and obedience of an elephant. This story effectively reveals the fallaciousness of his father's views.

Not only were John Lockwood Kipling's views on Indian religion and art lacking in insight, but his opinion of Indian national-

[7] John Lockwood Kipling, *Beast and Man in India,* 239.
[8] *Ibid.,* 240–41.

19

istic demands for self-government was also shortsighted. In W. S. Blunt's *My Diaries*, we read:

> Today old Kipling, Rudyard's father, came to dinner and I had a long talk with him about India. I wanted to find out from him, a typical Anglo-Indian, what remedy he would apply to the present condition of things. Like all the rest, he has no remedy to propose beyond "severe repression" for the time being, though he does not pretend that will cure the disease. He puts down as its causes (1) The Japanese Victories (2) Education and (3) Official lack of time to be polite.[9]

Rudyard Kipling inherited his father's condescending attitude toward the Indian native, an attitude he was to develop more fully and elaborately, almost into a religion. While critics like Edmund Wilson[10] and more recently Henry L. Varley[11] have attributed Kipling's superior attitude toward India to his school days at Westward Ho, they have neglected the impact of his own father in shaping his opinions. Kipling's admiration for his father amounted to hero-worship. That the elder Kipling had an equally high opinion of his son is obvious in his references to Rudyard in *Beast and Man in India*.

Rudyard Kipling was born in Bombay, India, on December 30, 1865. Surrounded by Indian servants whose native stories and nursery songs he heard, he began to think and feel in the Indian tongue. Some of these early years in India are recaptured in his autobiography:

> In the afternoon heats before we took our sleep, she or Mehta would tell us stories and Indian nursery songs all unforgotten, and we were sent into the dining room after we had been dressed, with the caution, "Speak English now to Papa and Mamma." So one spoke "English," haltingly translated out of the vernacular idiom that one thought and dreamed in![12]

9 *My Diaries, 1888–1914*, II, 211.
10 "The Kipling That Nobody Read," *The Wound and the Bow*, 118–19.
11 "Imperialism and Rudyard Kipling," *Journal of the History of Ideas*, Vol. XIV (January 1953), 124–25.
12 *Something of Myself*, 5.

No other Anglo-Indian writer uses Indian words with Kipling's ease and understanding. His use of them came from immediate experience, not secondhand, and many of the Indian words used in *Barrack Room Ballads* have become part of the English language. Edmund Wilson writes that Kipling even looked like an Indian as a young boy: "A drawing of him made by a school mate shows a swarthy boy with lank straight hair, who might almost pass for a Hindu."[13] According to this drawing, Kipling looked like his later hero *Kim*.

The young Kipling was fascinated by the colorful picturesqueness of the Indian fruit markets, the palm groves by the sea, and the gaily colored Parsees. As a child he often wandered into his father's school of art, where he lingered amidst the smells of paints and oils and played with lumps of clay. Observant and impressionable as the child was, these early surroundings helped create the picture of India as colorful, bright, and exotic. The strangeness of it contributed to the romantic atmosphere of his early days. Along with the color and gaiety, elements of force and violence also existed in India. Near Kipling's home were the towers of silence, where the Parsees offered their dead to the vultures. We read in *Something of Myself* that one day Kipling saw a child's hand lying in the family's garden. He could remember the assassination of Lord Mayo. Disturbing Kipling's happy childhood world of colors and dreams, these memories help to explain his divided attitude, partly romantic and partly realistic, in his writings about India.

After six pleasant years of childhood in India, Kipling and his sister were sent to England to a relative of their father. This woman, under whose supervision the children lived for six years in what Kipling calls "The House of Desolation," possessed a strong streak of sadism. Kipling recorded the sad and lonely experiences of this period in the early part of *The Light that Failed* and in "Baa, Baa, Black Sheep." These tortured years produced a distorted picture of the world, a world bereft of love, faith, and kindness. We cannot agree, however, when Edmund Wilson writes that, as a result of these harrowing experiences, "Kipling's

[13] *The Wound and the Bow*, 107.

C.1

The Emmet O'Neal Library
Mountain Brook, Alabama

entire life was to be shot through with hatred."[14] His Indian periods, both the early six years and the later years he spent in India as a journalist, show no hatred, although revealing strong dislikes and prejudices. In contrast to this time in England the early years in India stood out happy and memorable.

Next Kipling went to study at the United Services College at Westward Ho! This was a public school designed for children whose families had a military background or were connected with work for the government. From January, 1878, to July, 1882, Kipling stayed at this school; his experiences there are reflected in *Stalky and Co.* In the "House of Desolation," Kipling's compensatory reading in dark corners had injured his eyesight. Thus his participation in the more vigorous athletic activities of the school was limited, though he held his own in sharpness of mind. Cormell Price, the headmaster, designated Kipling as editor of the school newspaper, *The United Services College Chronicle.* Most of the poems which he contributed to this paper were youthful parodies of Browning and Swinburne, or doggerel narratives of boys' adventures. One poem, in the eighth number (March 20, 1882), is more significant. This is "Ave Imperatrix" which reverently greets Queen Victoria at the time she escaped one of the several attempts to assassinate her:

> Such greetings as should come from those
> Whose fathers faced the sepoy hordes,
> Or served You in their Russian snows
> And, dying left their sons their swords.
>
> And some of us have fought for You
> Already in the Afghan pass
> Or where the scarce-seen smoke puffs flew
> From Boer marksmen in the grass;
>
> And all are bred to do Your will
> By land and sea wherever flies
> The flag to fight and follow still
> And work Your Empire's destinies.[15]

14 *Ibid.*
15 *Early Verse*, 58.

This is not merely a conventional heroic greeting, but expresses a sincere note of patriotism, making reference to the expansion of the Empire and its destiny to rule the world.

Kipling makes fun of mere flag waving in "The Flag of Their Country" in *Stalky and Co*. Beresford, the M'Turk of *Stalky and Co.*, stated later that Kipling did not imbibe his imperialism at the school.[16] Nevertheless, the atmosphere of the school must have contributed a share, since many of the boys came from families serving the Empire. There was also constant talk among the boys about joining either the army or else the civil service for the glory of God, Queen, and country, with the result that they regarded themselves as potential empire-builders. Hence one is inclined to agree with Somervell when he writes:

> For Kipling the school is a nursery of soldiers and Empire-builders. "Just imagine," says the Beetle, "Stalky let loose on the south side of Europe with a sufficiency of Sikhs and reasonable prospect of loot." To which the infant replies: "You're too much of an optimist, Beetle."[17]

When Kipling returned to India on October 18, 1882, he brought with him a strong desire to write and a mind conditioned by imperialistic tendencies. Of this trip to India, which proved to be the most fruitful of his Indian years, Kipling tells us in his autobiography, "My English years fell away, nor ever, I think, came back in full strength."[18] He returned to Sussex later, as recorded in the sentimental poem "Sussex" (1902); but when he says, "My English years fell away," we must understand that he is speaking about his literary capability of using England and English topics as themes in his writing. He could never write as fascinatingly about England as he could about India. Life in India, as he described it, was new to the English reader, and he exploited this novelty to the full. Furthermore Kipling was primarily a journalist, deeply involved in contemporary affairs. In later life he wrote about England's past; most of these stories, collected in the volume

[16] *Kipling Journal*, No. 1 (March 1927), 17.
[17] *English Thought in the Nineteenth Century*, 187.
[18] *Something of Myself*, 45.

entitled *Rewards and Fairies* (1912), make very dull reading. None occupies a prominent place among his more popular stories, all of which are Indian tales. India was his territory; here he achieved recognition as a writer, with Englishmen swearing by Kipling on Indian matters. The return to Sussex and to English years was only a return to settle down, to rest and bask in the prosperity and fame that he had earned in India. India was the place for labor, Sussex the place for enjoyment of the fruits of his labor.

Kipling had seen his work in print even before he came back to India. Apart from his editorship of the school newspaper and his contributions to *The Scribbler,* a child's paper edited by the two daughters of William Morris, he had been sending his verses to his father in India. John Lockwood Kipling had fifty copies run off the press of *The Civil and Military Gazette* in 1881, under the title *Schoolboy Lyrics.* Both of Kipling's parents were contributing to Indian newspapers. Kipling, Sr., was the Bombay correspondent for *The Pioneer,* and Mrs. Kipling was writing letters from Simla to the same paper. They were, furthermore, prominent and influential members of Lahore society. Thus when the problem arose of finding the young Kipling a career in India, there was no difficulty in getting him a job as "assistant editor" on *The Civil and Military Gazette* of Lahore.

Although Kipling was barely eighteen, he occupied a position of importance in India as a journalist. As he writes in *Something of Myself:*

> I had my own room in the house; my servant, handed over to me by my father's servant, whose son he was, with the solemnity of a marriage contract; my own horse, cart, and groom; my own office hours and direct responsibilities . . . . We delighted more in each other's society than in that of strangers; and when my sister came out, a little later, our cup was filled to the brim. Not only were we happy, but we knew it.[19]

In Lahore and Simla he had the constant advice of his parents and sister, who were the first sympathetic and critical audience for his

[19] *Ibid.,* 46.

literary work. They also joined in writing with him. *Echoes—By Two Writers*, for example, was a joint effort by Kipling and his sister, published in 1884. In 1885, the entire family joined forces in *Quartette*, the Christmas annual of *The Civil and Military Gazette*, by four Anglo-Indian writers. From the four prose contributions by young Kipling two have found a permanent place among his best known stories, "The Phantom Rickshaw" and "The Strange Ride of Morrowbie Jukes, C.E."

Kipling worked hard in India and wrote his Indian tales and verse in a happy frame of mind, an especially important factor in evaluating his interpretations. Yet there does not emerge from his stories a happy or pleasant picture of India. His first two Indian tales, "The Phantom Rickshaw" and "The Strange Ride of Morrowbie Jukes, C.E.," are both horror tales. With the exception of *Kim*, written many years after Kipling had left India, all his stories present a tortured vision of the country. After leaving, Kipling was lonely for India, which he had come to consider his "home." Many of his later tales written in England reflect this feeling. Hilton Brown supports such a view when he writes of Rudyard Kipling:

> Perhaps India was the one place (with the possible exception of France of which he has written but meagrely) where he felt completely at home. In Vermont he had infinite good intention, he acquired the patois, he soaked in the local colour; but felt himself among foreigners. South Africa was permanently shadowed by the cloud of that Boer War which had shaken so many hitherto unquestioned axioms. Sussex becomes at times a little shrill and the hymn of its praise determined to the verge of protestation. But in India there was accord.[20]

The question naturally arises: if Kipling had a pleasant life and if he loved India, why then should his Indian writings present a tortured vision of reality? The answer is not difficult to find and provides a clue to an understanding of the nature of his mind.

There existed for Kipling two Indias. First, there was the per-

[20] *Rudyard Kipling*, 39.

sonal India of his liking, which provided him with material comforts, "carriage and servants," and literary fame. This was the India where the presence of his family radiated warmth and affection and gave him personal security. He felt at home, for there existed the "accord" described by Hilton Brown. Then there was colonial India. Of this the Bishop of Oxford wrote, "God has entrusted India to us to hold it for Him, and we have no right to give it up."[21] This was the India that provided Kipling with tales, for he was the chronicler of colonial India. In such writing, however, he had a specific purpose—to impress upon the minds of Englishmen at home the almost divine necessity of maintaining the British Empire. In his writings he was to interpret with greater zest the words of the Bishop of Oxford. He realized that to present this idea forcefully, he must portray the heroism and self-sacrifice of Englishmen working in India for the empire. He wanted to show that theirs was not an easy task, for they had to battle against superstition and violence and had to deal with "the lesser breed without the law."[22] Kipling glorified the empire-builder, whose excellence increased with corresponding emphasis on the strange and uncongenial environment in which he had to carry out his task. Thus, in his obsession with conversion of followers to the cause of the empire, he suppressed his own personal preference in the interests of what he considered the greater cause. In so doing, he was following the English public-school tradition, in which he implicitly believed:

> The game is more than the player of the game,
> And the ship is more than the crew![23]

His Indian writings, therefore, are politically motivated to serve the cause of the empire. He excluded the normal life of India from his picture, and by emphasizing and sometimes even creating sensational incidents and characters, he was able to fashion an impressive background for British achievement. His later writings

21 Richard Congreve, *India, a Pamphlet Published in 1857* (London, 1907), 14.
22 "Recessional," *Rudyard Kipling's Verse*, 327.
23 "A Song in Storm," *ibid.*, 147.

26

show a more pleasant picture of India, as is evidenced by *Kim* and by some of the tales in the two *Jungle Books*. Such a presentation was possible later in life, for his Indian experiences had mellowed and he had matured to some extent. He was able to look at India objectively.

On the *Civil and Military Gazette*, Kipling worked under Stephen Wheeler, the two comprising the entire editorial staff of a paper that kept 160 native compositors at work.[24] Since Wheeler did not greatly appreciate his partner's work, often the latter's duties as assistant editor were far from literary in nature. They consisted of preparing for the press all telegrams of the day, providing extracts and paragraphs from other English newspapers, furnishing suitable headings for official reports, reporting all sports and local activities, and correcting all proofs except editorial matter.[25] One of the privileges Kipling enjoyed was the freedom to submit articles refused by *The Civil and Military Gazette* in Lahore to other papers for publication. Sometimes these articles were not only accepted but paid for as well.

Kipling stayed on the staff of *The Civil and Military Gazette* from 1883 to late 1887, when he went to Allahabad as assistant editor of the Allahabad *Pioneer*, although he continued to publish in the Lahore paper. Finally there were four papers in which his writings appeared. The first was *The Civil and Military Gazette*; the second, *The Pioneer* of Allahabad; and the third and fourth were off-print papers of *The Pioneer*, called *The Pioneer Mail* and *The Week's News* respectively. *The Pioneer Mail* was not a regular paper, but was published only when direct mail operated between Bombay and London. It made use of material already published and hence was a scissors-and-paste production. *The Week's News*, a publication also making use of already-published material, added an editorial and contained either a story by Kipling or a syndicated short story or novel by Bret Harte. Infrequently, Kipling published in two other organs *The Calcutta Review* and *The*

[24] A. P. Cooper, *Rudyard Kipling* (Garden City, 1936), 6.
[25] E. Kay Robinson, "Kipling as a Journalist," *Academy* (London), Vol. IV (March 18, 1899), 285.

Indian Planter's Gazette. He also sent an occasional poem or tale to *The Westward Ho! Chronicle*.[26]

During the eleven-year interval between Kipling's departure from India in 1871 and his return in 1882, the country had changed rapidly. With Gladstone's full support, Lord Ripon had come out as viceroy in 1880 to implement a more liberal policy. The Afghan wars were over, and the Russian menace to the northwest frontier was growing. New railways linked parts of the country, and several good roads had been built. With the annexation of Upper Burma in 1886, the British conquest of Burma was complete. Famines still occurred, but a famine commission had been set up to deal with, or at least minimize, these disasters. Simla, because it had become the summer capital of the government, assumed a new importance.

Kipling's awareness of these happenings is evident in his writings. His "Ballad of Boh Da Thone" (1888) is about the Burma War of 1883–85. There is a reference to the famine commission in the story "William, the Conqueror," while "The Ballad of the King's Mercy" and "The Ballad of the King's Jest" center on the life of the tough Afghans. *Departmental Ditties* and the tales about Mrs. Hauksbee in *Plain Tales from the Hills* satirize the intrigue and superficiality of life in high society as it revolved around the summer capital. "The Man Who Was," concerning the Russian spy Dirkovitch, touches upon the increasing Russian menace to the northwest frontier provinces. In *Kim*, the Russian threat to the security of India provides the element of intrigue and the opportunity for Kim to learn the secrets of the "Great Game."

But there were other important events which Kipling failed either to observe or to understand. In the conflict between the "Orientalists" (advocating a more vigorous pursuit of Sanskrit, Persian, and Arabic studies) and the "Anglicists" (advocating the imparting of liberal education on Western lines through the medium of English), the latter won the day, and English education became the basis for Indian educational policy. It also opened new

[26] Flora Livingston, *Bibliography of the Works of Rudyard Kipling*, 102; and *Supplement*, 102.

doors to Western thought and linked India with the world of modern science and technology. Since the advantages of English education were reaped mostly by the middle-class Hindus, it resulted in the growth of an educated middle class.

English education qualified Indians to participate in the administration of the country and inspired them with those liberal ideas exemplified in the Catholic Emancipation Act (1829), the Reform Bill (1832), the Abolition of Slavery (1833), and the New Poor Law (1834). Many schools and colleges were set up; the vernacular press, recognizing its potentiality for influencing public opinion, was progressing in that direction. Education also made the Indians critical of British rule. The Indian press was so outspoken that Lord Lytton had to impose the Vernacular Press Act in 1878, to restrict and control its activities. Although Ripon repealed this act of censorship, it was reinstated in 1908. Queen Victoria's promise in 1858 of increasing opportunities for Indians to participate in the civil service was not followed in practice. There was considerable agitation for increased Indian participation in the internal administration of the country. To this was added discontent over the limitation of freedom of expression in the Press Act and the curb on personal freedom in the Arms Act, which prohibited Indians from carrying arms. These repressive measures were obstacles in the path of Indian national leaders. One result was the appeal made by these leaders for a permanent All-India organization to express the grievances of the Indian people.

The Ilbert Bill of 1883 was responsible for hastening the formation of such an All-India organization. This bill sought to bring about equality among Indian communities by permitting native judges to try European and British subjects. The Anglo-Indian community raised a storm of protest resulting in further bitterness between the two groups and formation by the Indian nationalists in 1885 of the Indian National Congress to further their cause.

All these native movements were strong symptoms of a growing nationalism, a revolution with an unsympathetic Kipling in the midst of it all. Although he wrote of famines ("William the Conqueror") and floods ("The Bridge Builders") and captured the wit

and gaiety of Simla society, he gave no expression to the underlying restlessness and the revolutionary tendencies that were shaping a new India. Kipling was aware of the Ilbert Bill—he related
in his autobiography that he was hissed by other European members
of the Punjab Club because *The Civil and Military Gazette*, with
its government contracts, had supported the bill.[27] In "Tod's
Amendment," there is a reference to the legislature and the question of land tenures, but no mention of the Ilbert Bill. The fact
that Kipling knew of the existence of the Indian National Congress is evident in his ridicule of it in "The Enlightenments of
Pagett, M.P." To show his contempt, Kipling brings forward a
group of Indians, none of whom has heard of such an organization.
However he regarded it, the congress was responsible for arous-
ing the political consciousness of the people, a direct result of
which was the decline and fall of the British empire in India, in
which Kipling so firmly believed.

The political, social, and racial problems contemporary with
Kipling did not receive adequate treatment in his writings. He
observed the surfaces of Indian life without showing any dispo-
sition to probe deeply. Thus Walter Morris Hart's judgment that
every visible phase of India appears in Kipling's writings cannot
be substantiated.

Kipling's first limitation in writing about India was his immaturity at the time he lived there. He came out to India as a boy of
seventeen and one-half years and left at the age of twenty-three.
He was excited about India in much the same way that a boy is
impressed with a new toy. He lacked the perception and judgment
to comprehend India's fundamental unity in the midst of its apparent diversity of culture. His second limitation was his point of
view, that of an Englishman belonging to the ruling class and be-
traying an almost unconscious feeling of superiority. Kipling was
always the judge, passing verdict upon something he did not understand, never the active participant or imaginative sympathizer.
Third, Kipling was a local colorist, which makes him the spokesman of one region in India, the northern part. His pretense of

[27] *Something of Myself*, 57.

speaking for all of India caused him to use broad, sweeping generalizations far from reality. Somerset Maugham in his choice of *Kipling's Best* stated that Kipling was intimately acquainted with the entire northwest part of India,[28] but we learn from a more recent biography by C. E. Carrington that his knowledge of the northwest was based on a casual two-day visit to that area.[29] Lahore and Simla are the only two cities in the northwest with which Kipling shows real familiarity, as he should since he lived in each for a considerable length of time. This is evident in the intimate and realistic portraits of these cities in *Kim*, as well as in the stories and poems dealing with Simla society. The northern part of India, which is the setting for most of his writings, was known to him only in fragments.

Kipling's knowledge of the southern part of the country was both shallow and meager. When he was in the south, he felt himself to be among strange people, listening to even stranger speech.[30] Like Martyn in "William the Conqueror," Kipling did not like the "unholy names" the southern districts had, "all 'Ungas' or 'Rungas' or 'Pillays' or 'Polliums.' "[31] Later in the same story Miss Williams exclaims about the south, "What can you expect from a country where they call a 'bhistie' a 'tunni cutch.' "[32] When Miss Williams had finished with "the South of Pagodas and palm trees, the over populated Hindu South" and returned to the north, she felt that:

> The large open names of the home towns were good to listen to. Umballa, Ludhiana, Phillour, Jullundur, they rang like the coming marriage bells in her ears.[33]

The feelings of Miss Williams for the south well may have been those of Kipling himself.

Kipling's audience was few but fit. *The Pioneer* had a circulation of five hundred copies, whereas *The Civil and Military Gazette*

[28] *Maugham's Choice of Kipling's Best*, 4.
[29] *The Life of Rudyard Kipling*, 46.
[30] *Something of Myself*, 112.
[31] "William the Conqueror," *The Day's Work*, I, 183.
[32] *Ibid.*, 208.
[33] *Ibid.*, 225.

31

had two thousand subscribers.[34] Between the years 1882 and 1889, eight books by Kipling were published.[35] Other writings belonging to his Indian stay were published later.[36] Both categories yield 142 short stories, published over a period of seven years. After he left India, A. H. Wheeler and Company, his Indian publishers, collected some of his minor pieces and published them without the author's permission. He suppressed these volumes: *The City of Dreadful Night* (1890), *The Smith Administration* (1891), and *The Letters of Marque* (1891). The entire stock, with the exception of three copies of each, was supposed to be destroyed. In later years, however, Kipling authorized publication of these volumes by making his own selection. *The Smith Administration*, already mentioned, contains some stories, while the other two volumes comprise sketches and views of Calcutta and accounts of Kipling's travels.

Kipling also had a considerable amount of poetry published before his departure from India in 1889. His leaving was the result of reading, in the autumn of 1886, Walter Besant's novel *All in a Garden Fair*. The novel tells the story of three young men in love with a girl whom they have known since a childhood spent together in Epping Forest. In the course of time the three young men go in pursuit of different careers. In the city, one of them becomes wealthy by ignoble means and loses his chance of marrying the girl. The second becomes a starving but dedicated poet, who in his devotion to his "art" forgets the girl. The third lover remains faithful to his love, returns to her, and thus wins her.

It is rather difficult to find, as Carrington suggests in his *Life of Rudyard Kipling*, the exact relationship that *All in a Garden Fair* had to Kipling's life.[37] There is, however, one passage in the novel which might have given Kipling the idea that, whether it was fame or wealth he wanted, he had to seek it in England and not in India. The passage concerns Will, one of the young men in Besant's novel, who feels that life overseas is not necessarily better than life at home:

---

[34] *Hubbard's Newspaper and Bank Directory of the World*, II, 1928, 1933.
[35] See Appendix, page 166 below.
[36] *Ibid*.
[37] *The Life of Rudyard Kipling*, 65.

"I am living among a most remarkable people, whose ways are not our ways. . . . Besides dancing, I have learned to ride, to talk without arguing, to smoke cigarettes, and to play whist. . . . As for adventures, there are none as yet; as for work, it is monotonous here as in England. I am like a knight who put on all his armour and went out in search of adventures and found none. I might as well have looked for them in Chigwell road."[38]

Kipling may also have felt that he was missing the larger life of change in England, and the feeling may have been aroused by a passage like the following in Besant's novel:

There is a thing concerning colonial life which is little comprehended. It is that ideas change slowly out there. The things which change ideas are the new discoveries, the new theories, the new men which are continually turning up at home. We who stay at home are borne along, whether we like it or no, by the current; we change our thoughts, our faiths, our standpoint, with the change that goes on around us. What is wild Radicalism one day is mild Liberalism the next. But in the colonies it is not so. One takes out a stock of ideas and comes home again with them practically the same, and it is not till returning home again that one finds how great is the gulf which a few years have made.[39]

Drawn by ambition to participate in the literary life of London, Kipling left India in 1889. In the course of his world travels in 1891, he made a brief stop in India, but this had no great effect on his writing. Thus, for all practical purposes, his Indian years come to a close in 1889.

Kipling's struggle for sheer existence in London and elsewhere after the abundance of his Indian years is captured in his autobiography, *Something of Myself*. The mood of these years can also be seen in the novelette *The Light that Failed*. While he had worked hard in India, he had enjoyed what he was doing. In London, joy was completely missing from his work. "The Finest Story in the World," a story written during this period, gives literary expression to his life of hard work, his sense of fatigue, and his mood

[38] *All in a Garden Fair*, II, 203.
[39] *Ibid.*, 210–11.

of depression. He chose the motto of the galley slave from the same story, "Oft have I wearied when I toiled at thee," to be carved on the desk that he used at Villiers Street in London.

In London, Kipling met Henley, their common dislike for Oscar Wilde in aesthetics and Gladstone in politics forming a bond between them. Kipling contributed mostly poetry to Henley's *The Scots Observer*, which later came to be called *The National Observer*. The poems that appeared in these pages later made up the volume *Barrack-Room Ballads*. Kipling came into contact with many literary figures in London, Henry James and Sir Edmund Gosse among others. He also became a friend of the American writer Wolcott Balestier, with whom he collaborated in writing his first novel, *Naulahka*.

After a world trip, interrupted by a bank failure, Kipling and his wife went to Brattleboro, Vermont, where they stayed from 1892 to 1896. To this American period belong the two *Jungle Books*, published in 1894 and 1895 respectively. Among the twenty-seven stories written in America, ten have an Indian setting. Two stories, "The Brushwood Boy" and "The Sahib's War," have settings in India, England, and South Africa. *Kim*, which concludes Kipling's writings about India, was also begun during this period (1892). He then turned to writing short stories about England's past. In 1916–17, he wrote *The Eyes of Asia*, published in 1919, which reflects opinions on the war by troopers from India. His last Indian story, "The Debt," is included in his last collection of stories, *Limits and Renewals* (1932).

Before these works are examined in detail, Kipling's basic attitudes about India and how he came to embrace them must be ascertained.

Kipling's life in India revolved around three different worlds. In Lahore, where he worked as a journalist, Kipling did not mingle with the Indians except when it was necessary for the day's work. His normal radius of travel was about six miles in any direction, and he tells us that "One did not meet new white faces at every six miles."[40] His first center of activity, apart from home and office,

[40] *Something of Myself*, 48.

was the clubs of which he was a member. These were the United Services Club at Lahore, the North West Services Club in Allahabad, the Masonic chapter at Lahore called Lodge of Hope and Perseverance, 782 E.C., and several army messes at Lahore. Of the last Kipling mentions the Second Fusiliers, the Thirtieth East Lancashires, and the Thirty-first East Surrey.[41] At these clubs Kipling met "none except picked men at their official work—Civilians, Army, Education, Canals, Forestry, Engineering, Irrigation, Railways, Doctors, and Lawyers—samples of each branch and each talking his own shop."[42]

The second world in which Kipling lived and moved was the social world of Simla. Simla, the summer capital from early April to mid-October, was the most prominent of the hill stations. Here Kipling came into direct contact with Anglo-Indian life, and from this experience came his satiric pictures of high society in Simla and his criticism of governmental affairs in *Departmental Ditties* and elsewhere. Most of the tales in *Plain Tales from the Hills* have a Simla background. In his autobiography, Kipling tells us about this new area of life and experience:

> Simla was another new world. There the Hierarchy lived, and one saw and heard the machinery of administration stripped bare. There were the Heads of the Viceregal and Military staffs and their Aides-de-Camps; and playing whist with the Great ones, who gave him special news, was the correspondent of our big sister-paper *The Pioneer*, then a power in the land.[43]

The Kiplings, particularly, became more prominent in Simla society with the coming of Lord Dufferin to India. The new viceroy was a family friend, so that whatever Kipling wrote caught his attention. Furthermore, Lord Dufferin at heart held the same views of divine mission and moral superiority which formed part of the Kipling ethos. In a speech given in celebration of Queen Victoria's Jubilee (February 16, 1887) on the Maidan, Calcutta, he made clear his idea of Britain's imperial mission:

[41] *Ibid.*
[42] *Ibid.*, 49.
[43] *Ibid.*, 63.

Through the *mysterious decrees* of Providence, the British nation and its rulers have been called upon to undertake the supreme government of this mighty empire.[44]

In another speech, made at Mansion House (May 28, 1889) in London on receiving the freedom of the City of London, Dufferin remarked: "I believe that the *moral ascendency* exercised by Englishmen in the East is becoming more and more powerful."[45] It is therefore not surprising that Kipling had great admiration for Dufferin. In Simla, the young journalist attracted the attention of important people in the administrative machinery.

The world of Freemasonry, with its ritualism, was the third world to which Kipling had access in India. In 1885 he was admitted to the cult of Freemasonry, "entered by a member of the Brahmo Somaj (Hindu), passed by a Mohammedan, and raised by an Englishman. The tyler was an Indian Jew."[46] Here Kipling came into contact with members of still other religious groups, for Freemasonry transcended all castes and sects. Yet, the members of the Masonic Lodge were those who held important positions, and consequently were a select few.

Kipling, then, lived and moved in an exclusive group of Anglo-Indians, and the few Indians he met belonged to an upper class. Because his servants were mostly Muslims, he associated little with the Hindus. Rather, he was surrounded by men of his own race, conscious of their achievements and of themselves as expansive, domineering, energetic, and freedom-loving individuals. These men of Anglo-Saxon stock possessed qualities, he thought, that made men supreme, and they lacked the qualities which held men back from material success. As supreme beings, they had a superior part to play in the evolution of the world and became, as it were, a chosen people with the mission of spreading culture in other lands. The Anglo-Saxon myth of racial superiority Kipling accepted, all too literally it must be confessed. It became the central cult of his writings, and he became the spokesman of the imperialist elements

[44] Marquis of Dufferin and Ava, *Speeches Delivered in India, 1884–8,* 160.
[45] *Ibid.,* 269.
[46] Carrington, *The Life of Rudyard Kipling,* 55.

of the Anglo-Saxon race, especially of the Anglo-Saxon community whose members he had known so well. He was always "the singer of the clan," of the dominant group as opposed to the nonconformist individual. "Kipling considers the individual," said Walter Morris Hart, "only for his organic value—as a loyal member of the team, as a link in the chain, a wheel in the machine."[47] Such a creed resulted in Kipling's emphasis on the social setting; his creation of character types, of typical military officers, civil officials, natives, and so on.

Kipling's faith in the Anglo-Saxon racial myth blinded his vision and regimented his mind. He delegated to the chosen race the onerous duty of civilizing a sullen people "newly caught," "the lesser breed without the law." In his adherence to this exclusive view, he failed to see the universality and all-inclusiveness of Indian culture. Dating from 2500 B.C., India has had continuous and living contacts with Iranians, Greeks, Chinese, and the Central Asians, and in later years with the Portuguese, the French, and the British, who brought in Western culture. India therefore became a meeting ground and melting pot for many cultural forces.

Yet Kipling, since he believed in the superiority of the Anglo-Saxon race, felt that the West and the East could never meet harmoniously, each learning from the other what it did not possess. When they did meet directly, the result was ludicrous. At the social level, such contact produced, in Kipling's view, a farcical situation, whether it was the Indian trying to become Anglicized or the Englishman going native. To illustrate his point of view, he created the satirical portrait of the educated Indian in the character of the Bengali, a product of both Indian and Western education, but not satisfactory in either. He was in Kipling's opinion a curious hybrid, who in spite of his Western education spoke poor English, mispronounced words, dressed clumsily, and remained still a "native."

Kipling, however, forgot to take into consideration the fact that the East and West were meeting not only socially but also ideologically and intellectually. While the Western-educated In-

[47] *Kipling, The Story Writer,* 10.

dian spoke poor English, dressed clumsily, and looked ridiculous in the superficial trappings of another culture, he was at the same time acquainting himself with the writings of Hobbes, Locke, Burke, and Mill. The concepts of democratic freedom and of government by parliamentary means caught his attention. He began to evaluate the West by Western principles and found that while England spoke of freedom and parliamentary government as her ideals, she never implemented them completely in India. Therefore, he became critical of the shortcomings of British policy in India; he started newspapers, within his limitations, to attack his own masters with what he had learned from them. Thus "it was a mistake to laugh" at these educated Indians, writes Hilton Brown, for "they were the first drops of a thunderstorm, the first echo of an approaching army."[48] The East and West had met, with the East challenging the West to give her more of the spirit of Western democracy, accept her as an equal, and consider her as a partner in the so-called process of civilizing her. Kipling, of course, did not even refer to such contact or to the dynamic events it produced.

The creation of an Anglicized Indian had been the object of British educational policy in India. Macaulay epitomized the policy in his classic statements made in 1835:

> We must at present do our best to form a class who may be interpreters between us and the millions we govern, a class of persons Indian in blood and colour, but English in tastes, in opinions, in morals and intellect.[49]

It is true that those Indians who had the benefit of an English education assumed the role of interpreters, but, at the same time, those who became effective interpreters retained their cultural identity. Western education made them aware both of the "dead timber" in their culture and of much that was good in Indian society. Most of the English educators, including Macaulay, had not realized that the introduction of English education would lead ultimately to a group of people who wanted to rule the country themselves, mak-

[48] *Rudyard Kipling,* 42.
[49] John Useem and Ruth Hill, *The Western Educated Man in India,* 14.

ing use of British methods but adapting them to Indian conditions. It has already been pointed out that John Lockwood Kipling attributed Indian unrest against British rule to the increasing education of the people. Rudyard Kipling considered the process of educating the Indian dangerous, although he ignored the significant political awakening and rising tide of Indian nationalism that Western education had produced in India. In doing so, he revealed his own limitations in understanding India.

The keen sense of personal security that Kipling enjoyed in India was also partly responsible for strengthening his Anglo-Saxonism. He saw and wrote about India from what Carrington, his biographer, describes as

> the secure base of a family life that was not only happy but four square and, it seemed, impregnable. . . . The family square made the only audience he cared to please. Let the world outside approve or disapprove. The family square could resist any external pressure.[50]

While the family square gave him encouragement and provided him with a sympathetic audience, critical of his literary technique but not of his views on India, at the same time it limited his contacts with values and ideologies other than his own Anglo-Saxon code.

It can be mentioned in this connection that Kipling was a voracious reader. Miss Weygandt, in her study of *Kipling's Reading and Its Influence on His Poetry*, bears out this statement by making an elaborate catalog of all the books he read. But we see no evidence either in his writings or in his biography that Kipling attempted to examine critically what he read. He accepted people and ideas that conformed to his way of thinking and dismissed those that disagreed with him or questioned his beliefs. His views were conditioned by his family, by his school, and by the heroes he had begun to worship—men like Dufferin, General Roberts, and the Lyalls. Bonamy Dobrée in a brief study of Kipling states that he never challenged ideas, but accepted them passively as long as they fitted into his pattern:

> He does not display the workings of his mind, his doubts, his

[50] *The Life of Rudyard Kipling*, 42.

39

gropings. He drives his thought to a conclusion; and it is only when it has reached the force of an intuition, of an assent in Newman's meaning of the word, that he clothes it in appropriate symbols.[51]

This was the mind that wrote *Plain Tales from the Hills, Barrack-Room Ballads,* and other verse and prose works about India.

[51] *The Lamp and the Lute,* 45.

III

The Anglo-Indian: the Exaggerated Vision

"There must be born a poet who shall
. . . compose the greatest song of
all—The Saga of the Anglo-Saxon
all around the earth. . . . Will
anyone take the contract?"
—FROM SEA TO SEA

SHORT STORIES are the center of Kipling's work; neither his poetry nor his novels possess the uniform excellence of his short stories. Somerset Maugham, in his introduction to a selection of Kipling's short stories, expressed the view that Kipling is the only English short story writer who can stand comparison with such masters as de Maupassant and Chekhov.[1] But Maugham, who lavishly praised Kipling's genius for telling a story, was not so exuberant in estimating his personality apart from his talent. Thomas F. Brady, who interviewed Maugham, recorded the following comments on Kipling:

> "Kipling was an imperialist," he said. "Remember that he was at the height of his fame when this country was at the height of its power. He was a very narrow-minded man and a very prejudiced one. I think his critics were right when they said he remained a school boy nearly all of his life."[2]

[1] *Maugham's Choice of Kipling's Best*, xxvii.
[2] "The Eighty Years of Mr. Maugham," *New York Times Magazine*, January 24, 1954, p. 52.

This indicates Maugham's implicit suggestion to approach Kipling purely for entertainment, discarding the views he enunciates. W. H. Auden in his poem "In Memory of W. B. Yeats," expresses the opinion that time has forgiven Kipling and his views, that his ideas are no longer largely accepted, and that he was confined to a great extent by the expansionist spirit of his own times.[3] Kipling the political propagandist is an essential part of Kipling the man and artist, the former often dominating the latter. This is evident in the conflict between the two images of India that he had, a problem we have examined in the previous chapter. In this conflict, Kipling subjugated the personal liking to the political purpose. Only in *Kim* is there more of the artist asserting himself than of the imperialist. Hence it is difficult to make a clear-cut distinction between the artist and the man.

However, we are not primarily concerned with Kipling's capabilities as a storyteller, for which he possessed a talent uniquely his own. We are concerned with a more basic issue of his writings, the question of his fidelity to the Indian scene.

The form of the short story conditioned, to a certain extent, his writings about India. As an assistant editor on *The Civil and Military Gazette*, he was commissioned to write on Indian topics according to specifications. Kay Robinson, the new editor, wanted to put some "new sparkle" into the paper, and Kipling was chosen to carry out this purpose. His writings had to be "topical, arresting, and short, restricted to two thousand words."[4] The short story met these requirements, but enforced limitations. For the "new sparkle" he searched out themes that were odd and strange, instead of the normal and the real.

As a boy fresh from England, Kipling was deeply impressed by the variety and contrast in Indian life. India's geographical immensity resulted in a bewildering maze of physical features. There were also many human varieties in the teeming millions of India, representing every race and culture. Nearly all the world religions, some of them claiming more than one million worshipers, had found

[3] "In Memory of W. B. Yeats," *Collected Poems*, 32.
[4] *The Life of Rudyard Kipling*, 61.

42

refuge in this land. He was able to see the impact of Western technology on an ancient, essentially spiritual civilization, producing an atmosphere of Old World piety with notes of modern progress. But what seemed most striking to young Kipling was the fact that a handful of Englishmen were masters of this subcontinent. He exploited these contrasts in his short stories, and by doing so he pioneered a romanticism of the present.

Kipling wrote for the average English audience, to most of whom India was just a splash of color on the map. As long as a selected group of officials kept the administration functioning, the average Englishman was satisfied. In fact, Thomas Babington Macaulay in his essay "Lord Clive" had criticized his countrymen for being indifferent to and ignorant about Indian affairs:

> Every school boy knows who imprisoned Montezuma, and who strangled Atahualpa. But we doubt whether one in ten, even among English gentlemen of highly cultivated minds, can tell who won the Battle of Buxar, who perpetrated the massacre of Patna, whether Surajah Dowlah ruled in Oudh or in Travancore, or whether Holkar was a Hindoo or a Mussalman. It might have been expected, that every Englishman who takes any interest in any part of history would be curious to know how a handful of his countrymen, separated from their home by an immense ocean, subjugated, in the course of a few years, one of the greatest empires in the world. Yet, unless we greatly err, this subject is, to most readers, not only insipid, but positively distasteful.[5]

Englishmen at home took no interest in Anglo-Indians abroad, according them no recognition whatsoever.

The Anglo-Indian families, described by Kipling as serving India "generation after generation as dolphins follow in line across the open sea,"[6] formed a circle among themselves after their return to England. These returned "Indians" were, in the eyes of stay-at-home Englishmen, men who had amassed wealth easily and had spent a life of luxurious ease in India. This was true during the early days of the East India Company. Ordinary writers of the

---

[5] *Essays on Lord Clive and Warren Hastings*, 1–2.
[6] "The Tomb of his Ancestors," *The Day's Work*, I, 125.

company were able, by private transactions and exploitation of the natives, to amass wealth with speed and comparative ease. Lord Clive and the grandfather of the novelist Thackeray belong in this category. But when the administration of India passed from the company to the crown, such exploitation was minimized, if not completely removed. Many nineteenth-century Englishmen, however, were unaware of this change in the status of the Anglo-Indian; hence the returned "Indian" civilians met with little respect and the soldiers with antipathy. Gordon Ray, in his biography of Thackeray, presents a graphic picture of these returnees:

> The humiliations thus endured by returned "Indians," whom half a life time of arduous service had sometimes made into personalities of formidable strength and eccentricity, gave them a detached and critical perspective from which to view the structure and customs of English society. Many of them asked the question that Kipling was to put many years later: "What do they know of England, who only England know?"[7]

Kipling was not only contemptuous of the "Little Englander," but enraged by his apathy. In the story "History of a Fall," Kipling presents the pathetic picture of Sir Cyril Wollobie, K.C.S.I., C.M.G., a former civil servant who in Simla had wielded power and commanded respect. On his return to London, Sir Cyril falls upon evil days and evil tongues. The story tells of his being jostled in a London omnibus with no consideration whatsoever for his previous services for the Empire. From a democratic point of view, Sir Cyril deserves no special treatment merely for having stayed in India. We cannot sympathize with his incapacity to adjust to normal life in London, but the story reveals the indifferent attitude of Englishmen towards those involved in work for the Empire. Kipling saw the Anglo-Indian as the underdog of the British Empire, who needed a spokesman to extol his virtues and restore him to a position of prominence and dignity. This was precisely what Kipling undertook to do in his short stories concerning Anglo-Indian life and its problems.

[7] *Thackeray, the Uses of Adversity, 1811–1846*, 67.

A group of English scholars, poets, and writers had written about India. Sir William Jones, John Leyden, and Edwin Arnold were great Oriental scholars and linguists who had devoted a lifetime to understanding the cultural heritage of India. Jones translated works from the Sanskrit, Persian, and Arabic, chief among which is his translation of Kalidasa's *Shakuntala*, and various hymns to Hindu deities, the "Hymn to Narayana" being the most notable. Leyden, an Oriental linguist, was a gifted poet and wrote several Anglo-Indian odes. Sir Edwin Arnold, in *The Light of Asia*, introduced to English readers the life and teachings of Buddha. But these scholars could reach only a small, educated audience.

Early Anglo-Indian novelists, including Sir Walter Scott, Taylor, Mrs. Steel, and W. D. Arnold, had touched upon aspects of Indian life that were totally new to the English public. Most of these novelists wrote historical romances like Scott's *The Surgeon's Daughter*, Taylor's *Tara*, Mrs. Steele's *On the Face of Waters*, Arnold's *Oakfield*, and John Lang's *The Wetherbys*. The strangeness and complications of Indian history had very little appeal for a foreign reader. The novels listed are highly documental, factual, and in that respect very faithful to Indian life. *The Surgeon's Daughter* reveals that Scott knew as much about the history of Mysore as he knew about English or Scottish history; yet the novel suffers from a lack of imaginative perspective. Arnold's *Oakfield* is critical of the narrow Anglo-Indian community, but digresses at great length into dull philosophical reflections. Taylor's *Tara* concerns the history of the Maratha tribe in the western part of India, with an accurate rendering of the manners, morals, and dress of these people; but his excessive use of factual details causes the novel to lose its aesthetic appeal. The Anglo-Indian novelists prior to Kipling lacked the capacity to humanize their situations. Interested in accurately interpreting the setting of their story, they sacrificed the moral and spiritual understanding of India. Furthermore, these novels portray Anglo-Indian life, and very little of native life enters into them. What there is, is confined to a few servants, soldiers, and an occasional Indian prince who is often cruel and venomous. Taylor is probably the only Anglo-

Indian novelist who attempted to portray the Indian native in great detail. None of these writers seem to have kept the conscious purpose of writing for a reading public. They made no effort to be popular.

It was left for Kipling to popularize India and her people. Such an approach had both advantages and disadvantages. It aroused an interest in India, but, at the same time, by concentrating on making a story "stand up," Kipling sacrificed depth and understanding in presenting Indian life. Making India his special province for interpretation, he developed a personal proprietorship about Indian topics.

In "Pagett M.P.," Kipling ridicules the "six month expert" who attempts to write and speak about India after a brief tour of the sub-continent:

> And I laughed as I drove from the station, but
>   the mirth died out on my lips
> As I thought of the fools like Pagett who write
>   of their "Eastern trips"
> And the sneers of the travelled idiots who duly
>   misgovern the land,
> And I prayed to the Lord to deliver another one
>   into my hand.[8]

Then there were the globe-trotters, men who do "kingdoms in days and write books about them in weeks."[9] For this species Kipling had nothing but contempt. In *From Sea to Sea* we find a picture of the globe-trotter outlined with great scorn:

> These eyes have seen him do it—master in five minutes the intricacies of the Indian Bradshaw, and tell an old resident exactly how and where the trains run. Can we wonder that the intoxication of success in hasty assimilation should make him over bold, and that he should try to grasp . . . ? But the full insolent of the globe trotter must be reserved. He is worthy of a book.[10]

There was also the young man from Manchester who was "doing

8 "Pagett, M.P.," *Rudyard Kipling's Verse*, 26.
9 *From Sea to Sea*, I, 3.
10 *Ibid.*, 4.

India" in ten days. But strangely enough, *From Sea to Sea*, Kipling's record of travels, was the product of globe-trotting by himself. But that, to use his own statement, is "another story."

Kipling, therefore, was aware of the fact that an understanding of India was not possible within a short period. He laughed at the popular conception of India that Englishmen had. In the short story "Yoked With An Unbeliever," he tells how Phil Garron, a young Englishman, went out to India and how his sweetheart, Agnes Laiter, wept because, like the rest of the English, she thought that India was "equally divided between jungles, tigers, cobras, cholera, and sepoys."[11] Phil Garron's mother was equally ignorant, and seemed to possess no curiosity whatsoever about the place where her son was going. Phil was going to Darjeeling, and Darjeeling to her was a "port on the Bengal Ocean,"[12] which is very much like saying that London is in the Mediterranean Sea.

Thus contemptuous of the "Little Englander" who was oblivious to what was going on in India, scornful of the globe trotter and men like Pagett, M.P., Kipling even accused the Indian government of superficiality in observing and understanding the real India. In "The Masque of Plenty" he took a thrust at committees set up by the government to investigate Indian conditions. They were official and formal, interested only in speeding up the inquiry:

> What is the state of the Nation? What is its
>   occupation?
> Hi! Get along, get along, get along—lend us
>   the information,[13]

and in returning to Simla with a glorified account that all is well with the nation, particularly with the Indian farmer, who is far from being satisfied, for

> At his heart is his daughter's wedding,
> In his eye fore-knowledge of debt.
> He eats and hath indigestion,

---

[11] "Yoked with an Unbeliever," *Plain Tales from the Hills*, 34.
[12] *Ibid.*, 35.
[13] "The Masque of Plenty," *Rudyard Kipling's Verse*, 35.

> He toils and may not stop;
> His life is a long drawn out question
> Between a crop and a crop.[14]

These lines present a very honest and realistic picture of the Indian farmer. Kipling's criticism of the government of India was therefore valid.

After pointing out the common faults of writers attempting an interpretation of India, Kipling set himself up as one who could really present India. He had great confidence in his capabilities, and in his writings we note a voice of authority, reinforced by the careful piling up of details for authenticity. We therefore await with eager interest what Kipling had to say about India, but unfortunately he disappoints us, for his presentation was equally stereotyped.

Kipling continued the old tale of the inscrutable Orient. He, too, observed the superficialities of Indian life and what he could not comprehend he called mysterious. If he had made an honest attempt at understanding, he could have found meaning in Indian life. The words of Lord Dufferin in the poem "One Viceroy Resigns" might very well reflect Kipling's attitude also:

> You'll never plumb the Oriental mind,
> And if you did it isn't worth the toil.
> Think of a sleek French priest in Canada;
> Divide by twenty half breeds. Multiply
> By twice the Sphinx's silence. There's
>   your East,
> And you're as wise as ever. So am I.[15]

Thus, instead of exploding the theory of the inscrutable Orient, Kipling merely passes it on, which indicates that in spite of his confidence about understanding India, he really had misgivings about his knowledge. It also provided Kipling with an answer to the charge that he could not comprehend India. He could never realize the words of E. M. Forster in *Abinger Harvest:*

[14] *Ibid.,* 38.
[15] "One Viceroy Resigns," *ibid.,* 69.

48

The East isn't palm trees and sunsets, or friendly rogues, or the Harem, or the cynical and discontented peoples, though it contains all these things. It is a spirit also, and though that spirit may not be the finest, we must attempt to define it.[16]

Kipling's short stories can be divided into two main groups: those concerned with the Anglo-Indian and those concerned with the native. The Anglo-Indian community consisted of two groups: the workers, who were actively involved in work for the Empire, including government officials, soldiers, engineers, and doctors; and the social or "smart" set, who lived, moved, and had their being in Simla. The native community was comprised of the educated Indian and the uneducated.

The Anglo-Indian was an image of the perfect Anglo-Saxon. He was efficient, resourceful, superior to others in physique and intellect, and, above all, dedicated to the task of civilizing the dark man. He believed in the "white man's burden." He accepted pain, exile, and neglect as part of the price he had to pay for belonging to a chosen race. He became a martyr to the cause. All who did not fit into this pattern fell by the way, but were quickly replaced by others who had implicit faith in the work they were doing for the empire. This was the picture of the ideal Anglo-Indian held up by Kipling.

In presenting the Anglo-Indian, Kipling had two concerns. He wanted, first, to win sympathy and prestige for those who conformed to the above ideals, and second, to satirize those who were frivolous, corrupt, and idle. By making use of the contrast between life in England and in India to evoke a sympathetic response for his Anglo-Indians, Kipling succeeded in producing an interest in them. Sir Edmund Gosse testifies to such a response in *Questions At Issue:*

> We see the ignorant and raw English youth transplanted, at the very moment when his instincts begin to develop, into a country where he is divided from everything which can remind him of his home, where by noon and night, in the bazar, in barracks, in the

16 *Abinger Harvest*, 270.

glowing scrub jungle, in the ferny defiles of the hills, everything he feels and hears and smells produces on him an unfamiliar and unwelcome impression. How he behaves himself under these new circumstances, what code of laws still bind his conscience, what are his relaxations, and what his observations, these are the questions we ask and which Mr. Kipling essays for the first time to answer.[17]

Kipling answered the questions that Gosse raised. But, even in dealing with his own countrymen, Kipling was exclusive, not inclusive. His Anglo-Indians were guided either by a stern sense of duty or by the frivolous motive of seeking pleasure. The Anglo-Indian as a person interested in being good merely because it is human to be good did not exist in Kipling's world. No Anglo-Indian character in the entire range of his creation expressed sentiments similar to those of Mrs. Moore in E. M. Forster's *A Passage to India:* " 'I'm going to argue, and indeed dictate,' she said, clinking her rings. 'The English are out here to be pleasant.' "[18]

Kipling's Anglo-Indian world was a world bereft of human relationships. It was in many ways a sordid and monotonous world. None of his Anglo-Indians were interested in music or literature or any other cultural pursuits. The women were eager for invitations to the Viceroy's ball and spent their time planning how to capture a husband. The ideal Anglo-Indians were too busy or too snobbish to cultivate friendship with the natives. Of course, "The Story of Muhammad Din" and the poem "Gunga-Din" may be cited to show that the Anglo-Indian official evinced interest in the native, but it must be remembered that in both these cases the attitude was one of condescension. Both Muhammad Din and Gunga Din were servants, and the typical feeling of a master for a faithful servant is revealed in these portrayals. The question is whether the Kiplingesque Anglo-Indian showed any feelings of friendship simply because the native was another human being.

By portraying the Anglo-Indian in these two clear-cut categories, the workers and the pleasure seekers, Kipling has done an injustice to his own countrymen. There were Anglo-Indians even during

[17] *Questions at Issue,* 269.
[18] *A Passage to India,* 51.

the life and time of Kipling who cultivated genuine friendship for the Indians. Many were sympathetic with the deeper aspirations of the Indian people. There was Hume, a retired Indian civil servant who founded the Indian National Congress; C. F. Andrews, a social reformer and a great disciple of Gandhi; and the editor of *The Pioneer*, Mr. George M. Chesney, Jr., who had an awareness of Indian views. In his *Autobiography*, Mahatma Gandhi writes:

> I had heard a good deal about *The Pioneer* published from Alla-habad, and I had understood it to be an opponent of Indian aspira-tions. I have an impression that Mr. Chesney, Jr. was the editor at the time. I wanted to secure the help of every party, so I wrote a note to Mr. Chesney, telling him how I had missed the train, and asking him for an appointment so as to enable me to leave the next day. He immediately gave me one, at which I was very happy espe-cially when I found that he gave me a patient hearing. He promised to note in his paper anything that I might write, but added that he could not promise to endorse all the Indian demands, inasmuch as he was bound to understand and give due weight to the view-point of the colonials as well.[19]

There were several others, maybe not so glamorous as Hume, Andrews, and Chesney, but nonetheless interested in fostering good relations between Anglo-Indians and Indians. But Kipling never left the official world to meet private Anglo-Indians.

Kipling's limited presentation of the Anglo-Indian resulted in a distorted picture. He presented only views that were favorable to him, and, as in "The Enlightenment of Pagett, M.P.," he scorned views that were disagreeable to him. In Forster's *A Passage to India* we find a Kiplingesque Anglo-Indian in the character of Ronnie Heaslop. Ronnie is the "Burra Sahib," the ideal white sahib that other Anglo-Indians of his type admire. He is their champion, ex-tolling their superiority. He tells his mother, Mrs. Moore, that she is above all natives except for a few ruling princes, and is their equal. Ronnie carries out in word and action those principles of official behavior that Kipling outlined in the story "His Chance in Life":

[19] *The Story of My Experiments with Truth*, 208.

Never forget that unless the outward and visible signs of Our Authority are always before a native he is as incapable as a child of understanding what authority means or where is the danger of disobeying it.[20]

Forster, however, presents not only the typical Kiplingesque white sahib in Ronnie, but also the sympathetic Anglo-Indian minds in Mrs. Moore and Fielding. Mrs. Moore, as has been pointed out, believes in the efficacy of good human relationships. Fielding likes the Indians, and when his countrymen express a desire to see "real India," he suggests that they see and mingle with the Indians. While Ronnie stands on the fringe of Indian life, Mrs. Moore and Fielding participate in it without losing their individuality.

George Orwell's *Burmese Days*, on the same theme as Forster's colonialism and racial tension, also presents different points of view. Ellis in *Burmese Days* is the hard-boiled, conservative Englishman who bears kinship with Ronnie in mind and spirit. He raises a great protest over the question of admitting Dr. Veeraswamy, a Burmese native, to membership in the club. In the character of Flory, however, we see an Englishman attempting to understand the strangeness and peculiarities of Burmese life. He condemns colonialism with its two accompanying evils of race prejudice and exploitation. Both Forster and Orwell attempt an objective presentation of different points of view, thereby helping towards a better understanding of the conflicts of culture and self-interests involved in colonial lands. Kipling lacked the challenging boldness to present varying opinions objectively. He created the Anglo-Indian in his own image, thereby failing to present him in his nobler aspects also, as Forster and Orwell have done.

Kipling's Anglo-Indian had an atmosphere of melancholy. On the one hand, the Englishman in India felt that he was an alien amidst a strange culture, while on the other, he behaved and acted as though he owned every acre of the country by virtue of belonging to the ruling class. Although he enjoyed the luxury and social prestige offered him as a member of the superior class, he longed for his English home and English friends. The Anglo-Indian

[20] "His Chance in Life," *Plain Tales from the Hills,* 82.

writer tended to emphasize the sense of separation from the home-land, with its accompanying spirit of loneliness. To this feeling were added the trials of being an exile, with the difficulties involved in the thankless job of civilizing a sullen race. All this resulted in the Anglo-Indian melancholy, providing a vehicle for the Anglo-Indian writer's expression of sentimental and romantic love for England by exaggerating the difficulties in India. The lines ad-dressed to his wife by an early Anglo-Indian poet, William Heber, may be taken as an example. He misses her companionship, and the strangeness in India is unbearable:

> If thou wert by my side, my love,
> How fast would evening fall
> In green Bengala's palmy grove,
> Listing the nightingale,[21]

But he concludes the poem with the devout resolution that he would hold on to the Indian soil, since duty commands his stay here.

Heber is mild in his expression of the Anglo-Indian melancholy, which increased in intensity and sentimentality with later writers. The poems of Richardson—"Consolations of an Exile," "A British Indian Exile to his Distant Children," and "Home Visions"—give eloquent utterance to the sense of despair born of isolation. Trego Webb, in his *Indian Lyrics*, expresses the quintessence of Anglo-Indian melancholy when he sternly accuses England of having made slaves of Englishmen serving in the colonies: "Thy slaves and not thy sons are we." Sir Alfred Lyall carries on this mood in his poem "Land of Regrets." He calls India "the land of regrets," a land of "trial and sorrow and woe, the land of tall black monu-ments and vainly proud sepulchral processions; it is a land that makes widows and orphans, that breaks hearts and drives men mad"; it is finally a land that puts asunder those whom God has joined together. This theme sounded highly romantic, often enveloping the poet with self-pity, which he exaggerated beyond the realms of reason. Kipling became a natural successor to this mood, which is strongly manifested in his writings, both poetry and prose.

[21] Edward Farley Oaten, *A Sketch of Anglo-Indian Literature*, 47.

The Anglo-Indian as an exile not by choice but by duty fitted in very effectively with Kipling's belief in an Anglo-Saxon race endowed with a mission and destined to martyrdom. The sentiment also appealed to his romantic sensibilities. While in India he longed for the atmosphere of England:

> I'm sick of endless sunshine, sick of
> blossom burdened bough.
> Give me back the leafless woodlands
> where the winds of spring range—
> Give me back one day in England, for
> it's spring in England now.[22]

But while in England he yearned for India in "Mandalay":

> Ship me somewheres East of Suez, where
> the best is like the worst,
> Where there aren't no ten commandments
> an' a man can raise his thirst
> For the temple bells are callin', an'
> it's there that I would be—
> By the old Moulmein Pagoda, looking
> lazy at the sea.[23]

"Christmas in India" describes the loneliness and sadness of the Anglo-Indian celebrating the festive season in an alien land:

> And at home they're making merry 'neath
> the white and scarlet berry—
> What part have India's exiles in their
> mirth?[24]

In expressing these sentiments of nostalgic yearning and a certain romantic agony in looking before and after, pining for other times and places, Kipling is making use of conventional ideas employed by earlier Anglo-Indian poets. Kipling himself may not have experienced these feelings of loneliness and moods of melancholy in

[22] Kipling, "In Springtime," *Rudyard Kipling's Verse*, 78.
[23] "Mandalay," *ibid.*, 417.
[24] "Christmas in India," *ibid.*, 54.

India, but he became the spokesman for his exiled countrymen. He had questioned in *From Sea to Sea:*

> There must be born a poet who shall . . . compose the greatest song of all—The Saga of the Anglo-Saxon all round the earth—a paean that shall combine the terrible slow swing of the *Battle Hymn of the Republic* with *Brittania needs no Bulwarks*, the skirl of the *British Grenadiers* with that perfect quick step, *Marching through Georgia*, and at the end the wail of the *Dead March*. Will any one take the contract?[25]

Kipling himself accepted the assignment.

In his zeal to defend the Anglo-Indian underdog, Kipling presented a dismal picture of his life in India. For those unacquainted with the country, he succeeded in creating the desired effect. The picture that emerged from his writings can best be understood by the impression it produced on writers like Gosse, who in *Questions at Issue* writes:

> In all these tales I am conscious of the barracks as of an island in a desolate ocean of sand. All around is the infinite waste of India, obscure, monotonous, immense, inhabited by black men and pariah dogs, pathans and green parrots, kites and crocodiles and long solitudes of high grass. The island in this sea is a little collection of young men, sent out from the remoteness of England to serve the "Widder," and to help to preserve for her the rich and barbarous empire of the East.[26]

This is as far removed from reality as Hollywood's conceptions of India. In India the Anglo-Indian enjoyed a high social position by virtue of the fact that he or she belonged to the ruling class. Life in India for many Anglo-Indians was much better socially and financially than life in England. Kipling himself, at the early age of seventeen, enjoyed a high social position, with servants and a carriage and entree to the best clubs. Yet he wanted to convince his readers that the life of the Anglo-Indian in India was full and strenuous.

[25] *From Sea to Sea*, II, 253.
[26] *Questions at Issue*, 271.

Kipling even had the viceroy of India, the supreme authority in the state, express the feeling of being an exile. In "One Viceroy Resigns," written after the pattern of Browning's dramatic monologue, Lord Dufferin hands over his responsibilities to his successor Lord Lansdowne, with a sigh of relief: "Well, now's your turn of exile. I go back to Rome and leisure."[27] Historically, this was not the case. Lord Dufferin did not consider his Indian viceroyalty as banishment. To the contrary, we find in Sir Alfred Lyall's biography of Lord Dufferin that he was disappointed that he had not been awarded the Indian assignment earlier.[28] Of all viceroys, Lord Dufferin spent the longest period in India, leaving his position only because he wanted to be with his children, who at their age needed the care and affection of their parents.[29] Lady Dufferin's *Journals* tell of the fascinatingly fabulous life that she and the Marquis lived in India. Lady Dufferin herself took an active interest in the social welfare of the Indian women. Kipling has a poem, "The Song of Women: Lady Dufferin's Medical Aid to the Women of India," which expresses in profuse terms their gratitude to the Vicereine:

> If she have sent her servants in our pain,
> If she have fought with Death and dulled
>   his sword;
> If she have given back our sick again,
> And to the breast the weakling lips restored,
> Is it a little thing that she has wrought?
> Then Life and Death and Motherhood be
>   nought.[30]

In *Naulahka*, Kipling presents a different situation. The novel records the unselfish work of an American girl, Kate Sheriff, for the women of India and their children, in the state of Rhatore in central India. But she meets with disappointment, for her motives are questioned, and suspicions are aroused that Kate may be a sorceress.

There is, therefore, a noticeable inconsistency in Kipling's pre-

[27] "One Viceroy Resigns," *Rudyard Kipling's Verse*, 69.
[28] *The Life of the Marquis of Dufferin and Ava*, I, 154.
[29] *Ibid.*, II, 138.
[30] "The Song of Women: Lady Dufferin's Medical Aid to the Women of India," *Rudyard Kipling's Verse*, 46.

sentation of India. While writing about Lady Dufferin, he was interested in paying tribute to her, which he did admirably by presenting her as beloved of all people. In *Naulahka*, Kipling was aiming to prove the point that East and West cannot meet. Thus the Indian women turn away from Western concepts of progress as embodied in the hospital and medicine. He forgot that he had shown them to be co-operative in a previous case. How India would be interpreted depended to a large extent on Kipling's objective at the time.

While it is true that the Anglo-Indian had his moments of depression and isolation, missing the cultural life of England, it is wrong to consider him a complete alien in the way Kipling presents him. On the other hand, with little or no participation in the administration of his country, hampered by the Press Act and the Arms Act and a victim of racial discrimination, the Indian became a stranger in the land of his birth. Yet Kipling makes no reference to the feelings of Indians under alien rule. Instead, he accuses India, an integral part of the empire, of treating Anglo-Indians negligently:

> Hard her service, poor her payment—
>   she in ancient, tattered raiment—
> India, she the grim step-mother of our kind.[31]

The Indian heat is another factor contributing to Anglo-Indian melancholy. Problems resulting from poor adjustment to the rigors of Indian climate, with its disturbing effects on the Anglo-Indian physically and morally, had been a favorite theme with earlier writers. Sir George Chesney in his novel *A True Reformer* described a railway journey across India to Bombay in the scorching heat of May:

> And now the day goes wearily on, marked only by the change of the sun's shadow, the rising of the day wind and its accompaniment of dust, and the ever increasing heat. The country is everywhere the same—a perfectly flat, desert-looking plain of reddish brown hue, with here and there a village, its walls of the same colour. It looks a desert, because there are no signs of crops, which was

31 "Christmas in India," *ibid.*, 54.

reaped two months ago, and no hedgerows, but here and there an acacia tree. Not a traveller is stirring on the road, not a soul to be seen in the fields, but an occasional stunted bullock is standing in such shade as their trees afford. At about every ten miles a station is reached, each exactly like the previous one and the next following. Gradually the sun went down, the wind and dust subsided, and another stifling night succeeded, with uneasy slumbers, broken by the ever recurring hubbub of the stoppages.[32]

From Henry S. Cunningham's novel *The Chronicles of Dusty-pore*, comes a similar description of Indian heat:

Vast plains, a dead level but for an occasional clump of palms or the dome of some despoiled and crumbling tomb, stretched away on every side and ended in a hazy, quivering horizon that spoke of infinite heat. Over these ranged herds of cattle and goats, browsing on no one could see what; or bewildered buffaloes would lie, panting and contented, in some muddy pool, with little but horns, eyes, and nostrils exposed above the surface. Little ill begotten stunted plants worked hard to live and grow and to weather the roaring fierce winds. The crows sat gasping, open beaked, as if protesting against having been born into so sulphurous an existence. Here and there a well, with its huge lumbering wheel and patient bullocks, went creaking and groaning night and day, as if earth grudged the tiny rivulet coming so toilfully from her dry breast, and gave it up with sighs of pain. The sky was cloudless, pitiless, brazen. The sun rose into it without a single fleck of vapour to mitigate its fierceness. All day it shone and glistened and blazed, until the very earth seemed to crack with heat and the mere thought of it was pain.[33]

Such passages could be repeated from practically every Anglo-Indian novelist, past and present. In earlier writings by Cunningham, Chesney, and others, the novelist deliberately created an artificial situation in order to describe the hot climate, seemingly a necessity in a novel about India. Kipling followed, incorporating such descriptions in his writings. In fact, he employed practically the same terminology as the previous novelists to describe the heat.

[32] *A True Reformer*, 28.
[33] *The Chronicles of Dustypore: A Tale of Modern Anglo-Indian Society*, 69.

In the story "At the End of the Passage," we read that the earth was dying of apoplexy,[34] which recalls the description by Cunningham that the "earth seemed to crack with heat and the mere thought of it was pain." The Indian heat provided Kipling with another convenient backdrop against which to describe the Anglo-Indian worker, who received a bolder definition by assuming the role of a tragic character fighting against primitive men and the cruel forces of nature. Such a picture could only come from a young boy who had had an overdose of reading adventure stories glorifying the Englishman as he fought against odds in the jungles of Africa and India. We must remember, Kipling was a boy of seventeen when he wrote most of his Anglo-Indian tales.

No one objects to Kipling's description of the rigors of the Indian climate, but to him it became a sinister force, an evil character, destroying his countrymen and making India the "grim step mother," "the land of regrets." Private Losson's tragedy in the story "In the Matter of a Private" and Dicky Hatt's motive for committing suicide in "At the End of the Passage" are largely due to the intense heat of India. "The City of Dreadful Night" has been written solely to describe the same, to communicate to the Western reader the "feel" of the "dense wet heat" which hangs over Lahore and other cities of the Indian plains:

> The dense wet heat that hung over the face of land, like a blanket, prevented all hope of sleep in the first instance. The Cicalas helped the heat; and the yelling jackals the Cicalas. It was impossible to sit still in the dark, empty, echoing house and watch the punkha beat the dead air.[35]

Rarely is Kipling's description of heat convincing and impressive. If we compare the above description of heat with that of Conrad in *Typhoon*, we notice that Kipling's becomes a traveler's note, while Conrad succeeds in getting the sensation of heat "out of his pages" and "into the reader."[36] There is, however, one good de-

---

[34] "At the End of the Passage," *Life's Handicap*, 244.

[35] "City of Dreadful Night," *ibid.*, 54.

[36] Alfred C. Ward, *Aspects of the Modern Short Story, English and American*, 121.

scription of the Indian heat in the story "The Man Who Would Be King," where it provides a very effective setting for the story:

> There are six other months when none ever come to call, and the thermometer walks inch by inch up to the top of the glass, and the office is darkened to just above reading light, and the press-machines are red hot to touch, and nobody writes anything but accounts of amusements in the hill-stations or obituary notices. Then the telephone becomes a tinkling terror, because it tells you of the sudden deaths of men and women that you knew intimately, and the prickly heat covers you with a garment, and you sit down and write.[37]

Such passages are rare in Kipling's writings. The inability of the Anglo-Indian to make climatic adjustments is deserving of sympathy, but Kipling grossly exaggerated the situation.

Monotony of official work also contributed to Anglo-Indian melancholy. The ruthless regularity and gigantic industry made machines out of men, taking the human touch away from them. It created in the Anglo-Indian sentiments which Ronnie Heaslop expresses in *A Passage to India:*

> I am out here to work, mind, to hold this wretched country by force, I'm not a missionary or a Labour member or a vague sentimental sympathetic literary man. I'm just a servant of the Government; it's the profession you wanted me to choose myself, and that's that. We're not pleasant in India, we don't intend to be pleasant. We've something more important to do.[38]

It was therefore a confirmed attitude among the official Anglo-Indians that politeness was something for others to worry about. As far as they were concerned, it was their duty to hold the country by any means, even by sheer physical force.

Wressley, in the story "Wressley of the Foreign Office," is a victim of the official monotony of work. Like other Anglo-Indians, Wressley did his work and grew to think it was everything and that he was the real pivot on which the administration revolved. At this point, "the curse of Anglo-Indian life fell heavily." He had

[37] "The Man Who Would Be King," *The Phantom Rickshaw and Other Stories,* 94.

[38] Forster, *A Passage to India,* 50.

devoted himself with religious assiduity to the complex entangled relationships in the central Indian states, thereby losing his sense of proportion. Thus, when it was rumored that Wressley was in love, it was both surprising and abnormal. But love inspired him only to do more research on the central Indian states, thereby causing his love affair to end in tragedy. Civil Engineer Moriarty, in "In Error," took to drinking, became an alcoholic, and committed suicide, all because of the monotony of official work. In "Thrown Away," "The Boy" also committed suicide. Practically all of the hard-working Anglo-Indians in Kipling's tales end as neurotic cases. They commit suicide or die or become alcoholics or go insane.

Kipling attributed all these freakish abnormalities and egotisms to the Indian environment. The Englishman before coming to India was all pure and noble, but strange things happened to him "East of Suez." He was not to blame; it was this land, India, which was responsible. Therefore, from Kipling's tales of Anglo-Indian life filled with heat, loneliness, official monotony, sordid flirtations, and official injustice, India emerges not as a beautiful or happy land, but a land of bitterness and "strangeness." Kipling's defense of the Anglo-Indian is acceptable, but when he attempts to win sympathy for him by presenting such horrors and abnormalities, he passes from realism to sensationalism. Edmund Wilson has admirably pointed out how Kipling later dwelt at great length on various aspects of neurosis.[39] Although his Indian days were free from want or hate, he seems even here to have been obsessed with the seamy side of life, which can only indicate that the early years of suffering in the "House of Desolation" were already coloring his views. We will have occasion to note later how Kipling's horror tales about India such as "The Phantom Rickshaw," "The Mark of the Beast," and "The Strange Ride of Morrowbie Jukes"—stem directly from his obsession with the grim and the grotesque.

"At the end of the Passage" is a good example of a story which brings together all the aspects of Anglo-Indian melancholy discussed above. The story has a verse heading which states and sets the tone of the narration to follow. The verse refers to the heat,

[39] "The Kipling That Nobody Read," *The Wound and the Bow*, 163.

dust, desolation, and sterility of the Indian atmosphere. The very opening sentence is cynical, and cynicism pervades the entire story: "Four men, each entitled to 'life, liberty, and the pursuit of happiness,' sat at a table playing whist."[40] Since these four men are in India, they have forfeited their right to "life, liberty, and the pursuit of happiness." With this introduction of mood and tone, the heat of India is again described in intense terms. The four Anglo-Indians, all engaged in official government work, are all under thirty years of age. They complain about the lack of bock beer and ice; heap scorn upon the comments of a Liberal M.P., made in an English newspaper, to the effect that the Indian Civil Service is "the pet preserve of the aristocracy of England"; criticize an Indian native state; and wish they had more hunting to do. A reference is made to Jevins, an Anglo-Indian mutual friend who had committed suicide a few days before, because of the dreary life in India. Jevins' tragedy is looked upon as an indication that death alone can liberate them from their Indian assignment. Spurstow, another Anglo-Indian in the group reminds them that "suicide is shirking your work." From this grim and desolate setting, Kipling passes on to the main tragedy, that of Hummil, the assistant engineer, who suffers from insomnia.

The intensity of the situation is increased by the fact that it is midsummer at the time of the story. Hummil's strange behavior is excused by his friends, for no man is to be judged by conditions in India. Gradually the story builds up to the point where Hummil cries out in deep anguish:

> "Give me something to make me sleep. I tell you I'm nearly mad. I don't know what I say half my time. For three weeks I've had to think and spell out every word that has come through my lips before I dared say it. Isn't that enough to drive a man mad? I can't see things correctly now, and I've lost my sense of touch. My skin aches. Make me sleep, Oh, Spurstow, for the love of God make me sleep sound. It isn't enough to merely let me dream. Let me sleep."[41]

Hummil's unfortunate situation symbolized, according to Kipling,

[40] Kipling, "At the End of the Passage," *Life's Handicap*, 244.
[41] *Ibid.*, 258.

the plight of all hard-working Anglo-Indians. When his friends suggest that he leave his post for a change of atmosphere, he refuses on the plea that such an action would be neglecting his duty. Kipling stresses spartan rigidity and sternness where duty is concerned. Hummil stands on the brink of insanity, sees his own apparition, for his mind and soul are tortured. The next time his friends call on him, Hummil is found dead on the floor. India has killed him. The friends look at his dead body, feel sorrow, but are immediately recalled by Spurstow to the business at hand:

> There may be Heaven—there must be Hell.
> Meantime, there is our life here. We–ell?[42]

"At the End of the Passage" is an intensely moving story. It has the brevity, the unity, the slice of life, all cohered with discipline. But as a picture of Anglo-Indians and their work in India, it is an exaggeration. That Kipling had a penchant for portraying tortured minds is further illustrated by the poem "The Galley Slave," written as a valediction to India. It presents once more Kipling's obsession with pain, hate, and torture. In the poem Kipling considers himself to have been a slave, recalling his servitude with fond memory, lingering over the many whiplashes he has suffered. He looks with pride on the mark of steel on his flesh, discovering thereby a spirit of comradeship with his fellow slaves. The allegory of the ship and the many voyages, with the suffering of the crew of which he was a member, is meant to publicize the work done by Anglo-Indians as a team in India. If Kipling's "Galley Slave" is sincere, then it must mean that these Anglo-Indians whose tragedy Kipling portrayed actually reveled in their pain and suffering. The lavish use of imagery in the area of sickness and disease seems to indicate that Kipling's strain of sadism got the upper hand in his stories of torture and disease.

In the story "Thrown Away," there occurs a tragedy similar to the one in "At the End of the Passage." "The Boy" in the story, an Anglo-Indian devoted to his work, commits suicide. A piece of hair belonging to someone else is sent to "the Boy's" mother.

---

42 *Ibid.*, 269.

63

Again, it is India that has killed him. His death is reported in a casual manner, suggesting the frequency of such deaths in this land of exiles, for this is, in the famous words of Kipling, all "in the day's work."

If an Anglo-Indian does not die or kill himself, he suffers keen disappointment because his work is not appreciated, in spite of the fact that he has taken great pains to "civilize the sullen race." Engineer Findlayson and his assistant, Hitchcock, come under this category. They are involved in spanning the river Ganges, which noble venture encounters several obstacles. The bridge, when completed, is to be a solid monument to British achievement in India. Despite the fact that many natives have worked on it, Kipling gives no credit to them, for Findlayson and Hitchcock knew "how the underlings were not to be trusted."[43] These two devoted engineers suffer the same as other Anglo-Indians in their effort to make their vision of the great bridge become a reality:

> The months of office work destroyed at a blow when the Government of India, at the last moment added two feet to the width of the bridge, under the impression that bridges were cut out of paper, and so brought to ruin at least half an acre of calculations . . . the heart breaking delays in the filling of the contracts in England . . . the war that followed the refusal. . . . Behind everything rose the black frame of the Kashi Bridge—plate by plate, girder by girder, span by span—and each pier of it recalled Hitchcock, the all-round man, who had stopped by his chief without failing from the very first to the last.[44]

All this reveals Kipling's knowledge of the delays and anxieties involved in official routine. His technical description of the construction of the bridge is equally indicative of his specialized knowledge. In 1887 he had given first-hand reports of bridge construction over the Sutlej on the Lahore-Ferozepore line and over the Jhelum at Chak Nizam to *The Civil and Military Gazette*.[45] He acquired a considerable amount of technical information about bridge con-

[43] "The Bridge Builders," *The Day's Work*, I, 7.
[44] *Ibid.*, 7.
[45] Carrington, *The Life of Rudyard Kipling*, 161.

struction to insert in his story. We are told by Sir A. Geddes in *Family Findings* that Kipling modeled the character of Findlayson on Geddes' father. Notwithstanding all the effort and patience that Kipling showed in the skillful construction of "The Bridge Builders," he was handicapped by his pet formula of making the hard-working Anglo-Indian suffer grotesquely. At the critical moment, when the floods sweep by, Findlayson takes a pinch of Malwa opium offered to him by Peroo the native, seeking thereby a temporary escape. He then suffers from strange hallucinations, seeing the gods of the Hindu pantheon. It is true that Findlayson does not suffer the same fate as some of the other Anglo-Indians, but even he, who has been presented as a sharply realistic and practical man, seeks peace of mind by taking opium.

None of Kipling's Anglo-Indians find peace of mind themselves or feel a sense of joy in the work they are doing. They protest, complain, die, commit suicide, turn alcoholics, become insane, or take to opium, never revealing for a moment any sense of determination or the qualities of reason and judgment that make an individual noble and dignified. Instead of emerging heroes, as Kipling planned, they turn out weak-willed and helpless.

Kipling presents an equally demoralized and depressing picture of the gay life of Anglo-India as it centered around Simla, the government's summer capital. Dennis Kincaid writes in *British Social Life in India:*

> In 1827 Lord Amherst had started the summer move to Simla. In spite of the difficulties of transport Simla soon became popular. . . . As the century advanced and methods of transport improved Simla became increasingly crowded with summer visitors, with secretaries and with those who hoped to be secretaries.[46]

Getting to Simla was therefore the be-all and end-all of Anglo-Indian existence. How to get there was the first problem, and, after arriving, how to remain was the second. The innumerable maneuvers, strategies, conflicts, and disappointments that followed in the wake of this struggle for survival in Simla, provide the theme for

[46] *British Social Life in India, 1608–1937,* 225.

a number of short stories in *Plain Tales from the Hills* and elsewhere. The men want to occupy key positions in the government; the women want to secure them for their favorite men. This results in flirtation, casual and otherwise. In fact, flirtation was part of the code of high society in Simla. One met people one would not see again, uttered sentiments one did not believe in, feigned protestations of love and loyalty which died on the lips as soon as they were uttered. It was all in the day's work. Kipling captures the spirit of Simla's gaiety in his verse:

> Eyes of blue—the Simla Hills
> Silvered with the moonlight hoar;
> Pleading of the waltz that thrills,
> Dies and echoes round Benmore.
>
> "Mabel," "Officers," "Goodbye,"
> Glamour, wine, and witchery—
> On my soul's sincerity,
> Love like ours can never die![47]

There is a feeling of recklessness, a keen desire to snatch moments of pleasure where they can be found. Dances, social gatherings, the tribulations of obtaining invitations to the viceroy's annual ball, the gossip, the scandals, the rise and fall of women presiding over Jakko Hill according to the bloom and fade of their charm and influence, set the values of Simla society, devastatingly pictured by Kipling. Commenting on these stories Somerset Maugham says:

> There is no sign that any of the persons he wrote about took any interest in art, literature, or music. The notion seems to have been prevalent that there was something fishy about a man who took pains to learn about things Indian. Of one character Kipling wrote: "he knew as much about Indians as it is good for a man to know." A man who was absorbed in his work appears to have been regarded with misgiving; at best he was eccentric, at worst a bore. The life described was empty and frivolous. The self sufficiency of these people is difficult to contemplate.[48]

[47] "The Lover's Litany," *Rudyard Kipling's Verse*, 230.
[48] *Maugham's Choice of Kipling's Best*, xxviii.

Kipling was so very satirical about life in Simla that it is no wonder that the people he satirized held him in contempt. In fact, some of them considered him a literary bounder, "a subversive pamphleteer given to criticise his betters."[49] Many of these stories written in the first flush of excitement are stereotyped and farcical. For example, there are the eight stories written in the form of a play entitled *The Story of the Gadsbys*. These stories concern the courtship, marriage, and honeymoon of an Anglo-Indian soldier and an Anglo-Indian girl. Captain Gadsby loves Mrs. Threegan, but finally marries her daughter, Miss Minnie Threegan. Mistaken intentions, a comedy of errors, and false sentimentality make the stories ridiculously farcical. Their construction, display of emotions, and attempt at forced laughter, clearly reveal Kipling's immaturity at the time he wrote them.

A similar theme of Anglo-Indian marital relationships revolving around mistaken identity is found in the story "False Dawn." Here Saumaurez proposes to the wrong Miss Copleigh, putting himself in an embarrassing position. "Miss Youghal's Sais" repeats the same formula: Strickland wins the hand of Miss Youghal by disguising himself as a *Sais*. Stories like "The Other Man," treating of an Anglo-Indian girl's love for the "Other Man" when she should have married someone else, or "Venus Annodomini," in which father and son worship the same woman, are brief, monotonous, and uninteresting. Yet these represent the type of story most prevalent in *Plain Tales from the Hills*. The reader is inclined to agree with Sir Edmund Gosse, who comments in *Questions at Issue:*

> I must confess that there is no section of his work which appears to me so insignificant as that which deals with Anglo-Indian society. But, as a rule, Mr. Kipling's 'Society' Anglo-Indians are not drawn better than those which other Indian novelists have created for our diversion. There is the sameness of the type.[50]

The sameness of the type is especially evident in Kipling's depiction of Anglo-Indian women, which to a large extent was colored by his own cynical opinion of them, expressed in the poem

[49] Kincaid, *British Social Life in India*, 230.
[50] *Questions at Issue*, 273.

"The Vampire." He expected of women the same devotion, loyalty, and efficiency in working for the empire as he expected of men. He therefore classified all women into two categories, "the pleasure seekers," who met with his scorn, and "the workers," who won his admiration.[51] Williams in "William the Conqueror" and Kate Sheriff in "Naulakha" are the only two women who belong to the "workers" group, thereby receiving Kipling's approbation. Most Anglo-Indian women in Simla belong in the first category. They are all presented as devouring females, social climbers, eternally plotting either to capture suitable young men or to cause their downfall. The story "Three and an Extra" may be taken as an example.

In "Three and an Extra" we meet for the first time that "little, brown, thin, almost skinny, woman, with big, rolling, violet blue eyes, and the sweetest manners in the world, Mrs. Hauksbee."[52] After three years, the Bremmils' marriage is falling apart as the result of the death of their baby, Florie. Mr. Bremmil, taking the loss calmly, goes out alone to a party and meets Mrs. Hauksbee, who "eyes him" and "annexes him publicly." This arouses jealousy in Mrs. Bremmil, who plots to recapture her errant husband. She discards her mourning, goes to parties, casts outraged glances at her rival, and plays up to her husband, regaining him just in time from the clutches of Mrs. Hauksbee. Kipling makes his point that "there is a woman at the back of everything."[53] All the tales about Anglo-Indian women in Simla are worked out in a similar pattern. Thus if the reader knows Mrs. Hauksbee or Mrs. Reiver or the Venus Annodomini, he has known them all.

In Simla, Kipling not only saw high society but also observed the workings of the government at close quarters. In the day-to-day administration, he found much to censure. He saw favoritism, red tape, and nepotism, to mention only the three most glaring defects. He saw inferior men getting along well, rising to positions of eminence, while more deserving ones remained in the lower eche-

[51] Bertha Campbell, "Kipling's Women," unpublished master's thesis, State University of Iowa, 1919.
[52] Kipling, "Three and an Extra," *Plain Tales from the Hills*, 10.
[53] "His Chance in Life," *ibid.*, 85.

lons. All this provided him with material for satirical verse in *Departmental Ditties.*

The style of *Departmental Ditties* was popular, even traditional, in Anglo-India:

> There is always an under current of song, a little bitter for the most part, running through the Indian papers. Sometimes a man in Bangalore would be moved to song, and a man on the Bombay side would answer him, and a man in Bengal would echo back, till at last we would all be crowing together like cocks before daybreak.[54]

Thus, while Kipling was using a popular mode in his satiric verse, he was also repeating himself thematically. *Departmental Ditties* repeats his favorite saying that whenever anything happens in Simla, particularly in winning governmental favors, "there is a woman at the back of it." Ahasuerus Jenkins in "Army Head-quarters" becomes a power in the state, because

> He warbled like a bul-bul, but particularly at
> Cornelia Agrippina, who was musical and fat.[55]

And Cornelia Agrippina, like Mrs. Reiver in the Story "The Rescue of Pluffles,"

> Controlled a humble husband, who, in
>   turn, controlled a Dept.,
> Where Cornelia Agrippina's human
>   singing birds were kept
> From April to October on a plump
>   retaining fee,
> Supplied, of course, per mensem, by
>   the Indian Treasury.[56]

Pothipar Gubbins in "Study of an Elevation, in Indian Ink," rises to power like the former Ahasuerus Jenkins, all because of his marriage to the proper woman; hence the poet asks the question:

[54] Jerome K. Jerome and Others, *My First Book* (London, 1897), 94.
[55] "The Army Head Quarters," *Departmental Ditties and Barrack-Room Ballads*, 14.
[56] *Ibid.*

Lovely Mehitabel Lee,
Let me inquire of thee,
Should I have riz to where Pothipar is
Hadst thou been mated to Me?[57]

Similar is the case with Ulysses Gunne in "Delilah." By reason of Delilah's marriage to "a gentleman in power," she was "acquainted with the gossip of the hour"; which she used to good advantage in seeking the promotion of Ulysses Gunne, who she favored. But when Ulysses lost the approval of the higher powers, she turned against him, calling him "a beast." Sleary, in "The Post that Fitted," marries Minnie Boffkin, the judge's ugly daughter solely to get a good post in India. After achieving his purpose, he leaves her to marry his true love, Carrie. Marriage was but a means to an end. Such are the themes comprising the greater portion of *Departmental Ditties*, sordid in many cases, repetitious always.

It has been said that most of these poems had enough basis in fact that persons could be identified.[58] They mean nothing more to us than casual verse written by Kipling to amuse himself and the people around him. That, in fact, was his purpose; there was no serious aim involved in the writing of these verses:

> They were made to ease off the perpetual strife between the manager extending his advertisements and my chief fighting for his reading matter. They were born to be sacrificed. Rukh Din the foreman would say: "Your poetry very good, sir; just coming proper length to-day. One third column, just proper."[59]

Written in the same frivolous mood that characterized most of his early Indian tales, *Departmental Ditties*, although repetitious, presents an inside view of the workings of the governmental machinery in Simla. There was a standing joke in Simla that one could not sleep there for the grinding of axes. Kipling elaborates on this joke in jingling rhyme in his verses.

In all of his work, prose and verse, examined so far, Kipling wrote about his own people, the Anglo-Indians. Before we turn

[57] "Study of an Elevation, in Indian Ink," *ibid.*, 17.
[58] *Life of Rudyard Kipling*, 63.
[59] *Something of Myself*, 74.

to a consideration of his treatment of native Indian life, we must touch upon another aspect of Anglo-Indian life, that of the British soldier in India.

Biographer Carrington, holds this opinion:

> He who wishes to know how British soldiers fight, how officers and men regard one another, how they talk the night before the battle, will seek the information in *King Henry V* or in *Barrack-Room Ballads*, for it is to be found almost nowhere else in our English classics.[60]

Kipling certainly presented a realistic picture of the British soldier. His hardships, his loves, his peculiar slang all have been faithfully recorded in *Barrack-Room Ballads* and in the volume of stories entitled *Soldiers Three*, concerning "the Three Musketeers," Mulvaney, Learoyd, and Ortheris. Kipling gave expression to the crude but true sentiments of the British Tommy:

> We aren't no thin red 'eroes, nor we aren't no
> blackguards too,
> But single men in barracks, most remarkable
> like you;
> An' if sometimes our conduck isn't all your
> fancy paints,
> Why, single men in barracks don't grow into
> plaster saints.[61]

Despite his realistic picture of the British Tommy, Kipling had very little direct contact with army life. Carrington points out that Kipling relied heavily on books and yarns spun by soldiers for his stories about British Indian army life. The story of the two drummer boys who saved the army, "The Drums of the Fore and Aft," is to be found in Orme's *History of India*; "Snarleyow" is an episode from Sergeant Bancroft's "History of the Bengal Horse Artillery"; "The Lost Legion" was a legend of 1857 arising from John Nicholson's punishment of the mutinous Fifty-fifth Native Infantry; "The Jacket" was an exploit ascribed to Captain Dalbiac,

---

[60] Carrington, *The Life of Rudyard Kipling*, 81–82.
[61] "Tommy," *Rudyard Kipling's Verse*, 148.

a gunner-officer in the Egyptian War; and "The Big Drunk Draf"
was claimed as his own by Lieutenant A. A. Howell of the Nor-
thumberland Fusiliers.[62]

In his tales of the British Tommy in India, Kipling was again
motivated by the desire to champion the underdog. Nineteenth-
century English public opinion of the British private was not very
flattering. Carrington has some perceptive remarks about the
situation:

> In literature, the attention he [the Tommy] got was confined to
> the professional heroics of the military historians, while amateur
> opinion was mostly based on Wellington's cynical remark that his
> army was recruited from the scum of the earth. Socially, the private
> soldiers were in fact drawn from the unemployed or unemployable,
> so that "going for a soldier" was, in the respectable working class,
> regarded as the last degradation, analogous with "going to the bad."
> Once enlisted and marked out by a uniform, the soldiery formed
> a caste apart and a caste of untouchables, living under conditions in
> barracks that were not even healthy.[63]

In the case of the Anglo-Indians, Kipling was motivated to win
recognition for them; his presentation of the soldiers was in a similar cause. But Kipling started writing about the Tommy at a later
stage. Everything he wrote about the army before 1887 deals with
officers and their life in the mess. Most of the stories center around
practical jokes, as in the case of "The Arrest of Lieutenant
Golighty" and "His Wedded Wife."

It is only in the stories about the "Three Musketeers"—Mulvaney the Irishman, Ortheris the Cockney, and Learoyd the dales-
man from West Riding—that we get a picture of the hard life of the
Tommy. These three first appeared in "The Three Musketeers,"
in March of 1887, and three more times before the year was over.
Kipling gave up writing about the "three musketeers," and took
up a new character in Gunner Barnabas. But Barnabas did not
make the same appeal that the three soldiers had made. Among the
soldier tales, the three best known, critically acclaimed, are "The

[62] Carrington, *The Life of Rudyard Kipling*, 80.
[63] *Ibid.*

Courting of Dinah Shadd," "On Greenhow Hill," and "Love O' Women." Written in England after Kipling's final departure from India, they deal not with the troubles of the three soldiers, but with their romantic life.

There is very little local color in these soldier tales, except that they take place in India. Therefore, the "three musketeers" could have been British privates in any part of the world and experienced the same hardships and privations.

In the treatment of Anglo-Indian life, Kipling was on familiar ground, moving among his own people, speaking their language and sentiments. In his treatment of Indian life he was stepping on different soil. Nevertheless, Kipling's work must face the challenge of critical examination in this area. India consisted of both the British Raj and the natives, the latter symbolizing the mind and spirit of the country. The next chapter will treat of native Indian life as it emerges from Kipling's pen.

IV

The Indian Native: the Tortured Vision

"India's a curious place."
—"THE ENLIGHTENMENTS OF PAGETT, M.P."

KIPLING possessed an identity of interest with the Anglo-Indian community about which he was writing. He was therefore expressing familiar sentiments in the dedicatory verses to *Departmental Ditties:*

> I have eaten your bread and salt.
>   I have drunk your water and wine.
> The deaths ye died I have watched beside,
>   And the lives ye led were mine.
>
> Was there aught that I did not share
>   In vigil or toil or ease,—
> One joy or woe that I did not know,
>   Dear hearts across the seas?
>
> I have written the tale of our life
>   For a sheltered people's mirth,
> In jesting guise—but ye are wise,
>   And ye know what the jest is worth.[1]

Such an identity of interests and sympathy with native Indian life was not possible for Kipling. Had he been an internationalist, which he was not, such a communion with an alien culture would have

[1] *Departmental Ditties and Barrack-Room Ballads,* 2.

74

been possible, however limited it might have been. But Kipling looked at Indian life with the eyes of a member of the ruling class, therefore seeing it from the outside, a fact to be remembered while examining his pictures of native India.

Kipling's preoccupation with the seamy side of life in his Anglo-Indian tales is repeated in his treatment of native life as well. Again it is a tortured vision. His Indian tales can be classified under two categories. The first group concerns itself with the illiterate Indian, the servants, the farmers, and the tribal folk. The second group centers on the educated Indian, particularly the Bengali.

Real India, or the India real to Kipling, was found among the illiterate people of the country; the farmer in the fields; the servant working for the "white sahib"; the tribal man close to the old primitive ways, and the hill girl unsophisticated in modern manners. In establishing the image of the real Indian in the personality of the illiterate, silent farmer or tribesman, Kipling was not totally wrong. His fallacy lies in ignoring the educated group of Indians as not representing the country. There was a reason for doing so. The servant class in India, together with the tribal folk, looked up to the white man with a feeling of reverent obedience. They were easy to control. In Henry Newbolt's "Ballad of John Nicholson" we read that the servant class had been disciplined to realize their inferior position, by making them follow even the minutest details of prescribed behavior and appearance before the white masters. As the ballad states, Nicholson and his few troops were caught in the midst of a furious Indian population preparing to join the widespread rebellion against British rule. He summoned Mehtab Singh, in whose loyalty he had faith. Mehtab Singh came to see him with his shoes on, an act of defiance, since natives were expected to appear barefoot. Nicholson whispered in private to his servant, "Take off, take off those shoes of pride. Carry them whence they came . . . ."[2] Mehtab Singh obeyed and walked out before his captains barefoot. He realized that he had forgotten his place and came back to obey the law from which he had swerved. This law, according to Kipling, was the law of Anglo-Saxon superiority in

2 Sir Henry John Newbolt, *Poems: New and Old* (New York, 1921), 172.

ruling others. He admired those who obeyed the law, and the "real Indians" were those who did.

The situation was different in the case of the educated Indian who critically examined British rule, questioned the Anglo-Saxon duty of civilizing half the world and thereby disobeyed the law which, to Kipling, was everything. He therefore disliked the western-trained and educated native in India, branding him a rebel and a reactionary. Nowhere else has Kipling made so much use of scorn, satire, and farce as in his portrait of the educated Indian. All his tales of Indian life are colored by extreme views reflecting an intense liking for one group and a violent dislike for the other. The story, "The Enlightenments of Pagett, M.P.," will best serve to illustrate this point and will also reveal the picture of India that Kipling was intent on creating for the benefit of his countrymen.

The story opens with a quotation from Edmund Burke's *Reflections on the Revolution in France*, which refers to the half-dozen grasshoppers making noise under a fern while thousands of great cattle lie peacefully under the shadow of the British oak. The comparison is obvious, for Kipling is examining in his story the importance of the Indian National Congress, which like the "meagre, shrivelled, hopping, though loud and troublesome insects of the hour," is causing unnecessary trouble. The remainder of the Indian population—the real India—basks peacefully under the British oak. This is the thesis to be proved for the benefit of Pagett, M.P., a Liberal member of the British Parliament.

Kipling, a conservative in politics, disliked Liberal politicians like Lord Ripon, the viceroy, and Gladstone, the premier, who, in his opinion, interfered with the existing order of things. They advocated increased native participation in colonial administration, sympathized with national native movements, and showed an interest in the democratization of British rule in India. Kipling distrusted the democratic process; as Edward Shanks points out, it "meant to him simply a system under which incompetent people strove to take work out of the hands of people competent to do it."[3] He was, therefore, an "authoritarian," making use of every

[3] *Rudyard Kipling, A Study in Literature and Political Ideas*, 91.

opportunity to satirize the Liberal reformers as totally ignorant idealists, far removed from the realities of British colonial policy.

In "At the End of the Passage" Kipling became sarcastic about the smugness of Liberal politicians. He created the characters of Pagett, M.P., and Mr. Groomsbride, two Liberal politicians, in order to bestow upon them his choicest words of scorn and contempt. In the case of Pagett, Kipling used a certain amount of restraint for making him appear naïve and misguided, with a talent for making a fool of himself. However, he descended to low farce in presenting Mr. Groomsbride.

Mr. Groomsbride makes his appearance in a short story, "Little Foxes." The scene is Egypt. Mr. Groomsbride is the Liberal politician on a visit to gain understanding of the natives. What "The Enlightenments of Pagett, M.P." does for India "Little Foxes" does for Egypt. By a series of incidents Mr. Groomsbride is made to look ridiculous, but the final blow comes when he makes a speech in the Egyptian native tongue, in which he innocently uses a certain phrase. "This short adhesive word, which, by itself, surprises even unblushing Ethiopia," sets the audience rolling with laughter, making Mr. Groomsbride the victim of a practical joke. This is one of the indications that Kipling never dealt with ideas nor presented an intellectual discussion of them, but resorted to cheap and meaningless situations to belittle his opponent. This is revealed by a closer examination of "The Enlightenments of Pagett, M.P."

Pagett, M.P., is on a brief visit to India, at the invitation of his former schoolmate, Orde, who, as deputy commissioner in the district of Amara in India, has become a cog in the wheels of the empire. Orde is one of Kipling's ideal Anglo-Indians, the devoted public servant serving God and Queen selflessly. Pagett wants to meet the people; know their problems; and examine in particular the new Indian national movement, the Indian National Congress. Orde acts as interpreter in helping Pagett understand India. Kipling speaks in the character of Orde, and the story is a strong defense of British rule in India. Since the story makes use of cheap techniques, playing upon emotional extremities, it is reduced to a mere propaganda piece.

It was customary for Great Britain to put on a show in India for the benefit of foreign visitors, newspaper correspondents, and Liberal or Labor members of Parliament. An eager desire to impress the visitors often led to a great deal of diplomatic contrivance in order to present the correct picture. People were carefully selected to present certain points of view, a liking for British rule, a dislike for native participation, expression of bitter racial prejudice among themselves—all to help in creating a picture of the English as "Protector of the Poor." The case of Miss Katharine Mayo, author of the notorious *Mother India*, is an example of how such propaganda operated, resulting in British respectability abroad at the cost of Indian dignity.

Miss Mayo, an American, visited India at the invitation of the British, to investigate the consequences of their rule. Her trip had many limitations. It was conducted, hasty, and therefore superficial. She had neither any knowledge of Indian languages nor of Indian culture, yet after her brief trip she wrote a book which received wide publicity outside India. Since it was a total condemnation of all phases of Indian culture, it created an adverse case for Indian self-government, thereby justifying British rule as proper for the country. Propaganda had presented a picture of the nation so horrifying that Gandhi, who rarely used bitter words, described Miss Mayo's book as "report by a drainage inspectress."[4]

The novel by Alec Waugh, *Island in the Sun*, which bears a relationship to the British West Indies similar to that *A Passage to India* has to India and Orwell's *Burmese Days* has to Burma, forcefully presents the use of propaganda in colonial issues. To the explosive island of Santa Marta, in the British West Indies, comes an American journalist, Mr. Wilson P. Romer. Governor Templeton is eager that the American journalist carry back with him a favorable impression of the island, so he sets the propaganda machinery in motion by giving a party and instructing his A.D.C., Archer:

> The colour problem is one on which the Americans are touchy. Mr. Romer must be shown that the various sections of the com-

[4] Beverly Nicolls, *Verdict on India*, 181.

munity meet on equal terms. The party today must not be allowed to form itself into separate groups of white, near white, brown and black. If you see such groups forming, break them up. I also want Romer to meet representative members of our community.[5]

The governor goes down the list of invitees, making out a list of people *he* wants his guest to meet. Romer is impressed, but the next journalist, Carl Bradshaw, also visiting Santa Marta, is not. He sees through the artificial picture created for his entertainment and for the benefit of the British, and he cables back to Baltimore:

> I sit on a volcano, one of the peaks of a now submerged range of mountains that curved in prehistoric days in a semicircle from the tip of Florida to Venezuela. Socially, politically, I also sit on a very live volcano here on the charming British West Indian Island of Santa Marta. I can hear its rumblings beneath me. Sooner or later there must be an explosion.[6]

It is against this setting that the story, "The Enlightenments of Pagett, M.P.," must be examined.

In spite of the fact that Kipling has attempted to make the several incidents look natural, the entire story bears the marks of deliberate fabrication at several points. The procession of Indians and Anglo-Indians before Orde and Pagett is extremely artificial. All repeat their prepared speeches, which are similar in form and content. Most of them speak in their native tongue, therefore Pagett has to depend upon interpretation by Orde. Most of these so-called "representatives of the people" appearing in the story are natives, walking right into the house of an English deputy commissioner. With no formality, they present their grievances; Orde listens with sympathy, asks them a few questions, and they depart. Such things as direct appeal to the officer did not take place in India, particularly in the year 1887, which is the date of this story. A deputy commissioner was an important official, a busy man, who could only be approached after expenditure of a considerable amount of time and energy, provided the issue was very important. Orde is represented as sitting in his house, meeting Indians as, and when,

[5] *Island in the Sun,* 82.
[6] *Ibid.,* 119.

they come. The Indian civil service, properly called the "longest red tape in the world," made the deputy commissioner inaccessible to the common people.

The first to come before Pagett is Bishen Singh, a carpenter, uneducated, and hence in Kipling's judgment a "real Indian." Bishen Singh states that he has never heard of the congress, and accuses the Bengali in the vilest terms: "Those black apes are far more efficient workmates, and for the Bengali Babu—tchick," spitting contemptuously.[7] Provincial loyalty exists in India, but prejudice, bitterness, and hatred such as Bishen Singh expresses are unbelievable. In considering this story, where Kipling's intention is to discredit the Indian National Congress, we must remember that although the congress was started by Hume, an Anglo-Indian, its early supporters were Bengalis. Surendranath Banerjea, a Bengali, was denied admission to the Indian civil service. This was in spite of the queen's proclamation of 1858 and the Indian Civil Service Act of 1861, both of which reiterated the administration's interest in increasing Indian participation in government. Mazumdar in writing about Banerjea says:

> Although he proved successful in the competitive examination, attempts were made to remove his name from the list. Ultimately, the name was restored by a writ of *Mandamus* in the Queen's Bench, and Mr. Banerjea was appointed to the I.C.S., but he was soon dismissed from the Service on grounds which are now regarded as inadequate.

> The man who was thus denied an opportunity to serve the British Government was destined to be the leader of the great national movement in India.[8]

A. O. Hume's letter requesting volunteers from among University graduates to form an all-India organization was primarily addressed to the students at the University of Calcutta, which by its geographical location in the Province of Bengal attracted mostly Bengalis.[9] Kipling branded the congress as a Bengali organization,

[7] Kipling, "The Enlightenments of Pagett, M.P.," *In Black and White*, 353.
[8] Ramesh C. Mazumdar and Others, *An Advanced History of India*, III, 889.
[9] Pattabhi Sitaramayya, *History of the Indian National Congress 1885–1935*, I, 11.

extending his own contempt for the Bengali character to include the entire movement. He also disliked the congress because it was started, as most movements are, by the educated community in India. Orde describes the congress as: "composed almost entirely of those of the literary or clerkly castes who have received an English education."[10] Furthermore, this story is supposed to have happened two years after the congress was founded in 1885. For a movement of this nature to spread to the entire people certainly takes a long time. Therefore, Kipling's condemnation, after only two years of existence, that the congress was the organization of a privileged class reveals his incapacity to see beneath the surface.

Bishen Singh and the twelve cultivators who follow him express pride in themselves and hatred of each other, thereby indicating to Pagett that the English alone are capable of ruling this land of diversity. One of the most startling passages, startling because it is so far removed from truth but uttered with such assumed confidence, is Orde's speech about the diverse groups in India:

> "Hate—eternal and inextinguishable hate," concluded Orde, flicking the lash of the whip across the large map from East to West as he sat down. "Remember Canning's advice to Lord Granville, Never write or speak of Indian things without looking at a map."[11]

This passage, more than any other, reveals Kipling's lack of understanding of India. To a casual observer, India presents a variety of people and places. But underlying all this diversity is a fundamental unity. There is the Vedas as the common source for Hindu religion, Sanskrit as the common source for most of the major Indian languages, the emphasis on a joint family system, a great interest in matters spiritual, a sense of tolerance making India the home of many different religious faiths—all these are part of the fundamental unity of India.[12] Kipling could not comprehend such unity, for he was superficial in his observation. He emphasized minor differences, presenting to a simple Pagett the horrifying pic-

---

[10] Kipling, "The Enlightenments of Pagett, M.P.," *In Black and White*, 347.
[11] *Ibid.*, 354.
[12] Radhakumud Mookherjee, *The Fundamental Unity of India, From Historical Sources*, 15–18.

ture of mass hatred among the members of the Indian community.

The people of India were moving toward political unity as the result of an awareness brought about by the Indian National Congress. E. M. Forster recognized this growing unity among the people when he had Aziz express the following sentiments at the conclusion of *A Passage to India:*

> Then he shouted, "India shall be a nation. No foreigners of any sort, Hindu and Moslem and Sikh and all shall be one. Hurrah! Hurrah! Hurrah for India! Hurrah! Hurrah!"[13]

Differences existed among the various communities, but there is a lack of proportion in Kipling's treatment of them. "The Enlightenments of Pagett, M.P." is an example of how minor differences were over-emphasized to increase ill feeling not only between the English and the Indians but also among the Indians themselves.

The twelve cultivators following Bishen Singh dislike all natives other than themselves, praise the British, and prefer English judges to Indians. Despite this parade of prejudices, there is fascination in the realistic picture of a Jat farmer's appearance:

> His strongly marked features glowed with russet bronze, and his bright eyes gleamed under deeply set brown, contracted by lifelong exposure to sunshine. His beard and moustache, streaked with gray, swept from bold cliffs of brow and cheek in the large sweeps one sees drawn by Michael Angelo, and strands of long black hair mingled with the irregularly piled wreaths and folds of his turban. The drapery of stout blue cotton cloth thrown over his broad shoulders and girt round his narrow loins, hung from his tall form in broadly sculptured folds and he would have made a superb model for an artist in search of a patriarch.[14]

Kipling was a keen observer of surface appearances, and the only valid interpretative pieces in his story are the occasional portraits of Indian people drawn with sensitivity and fidelity to external details.

Kipling's portrait of the Jat farmer helped his father make a painting of him for *Kim*, but the sentiments expressed by the Jat

13 *A Passage to India,* 281.
14 Kipling, "The Enlightenments of Pagett, M.P.," 362.

are not valid. The farmer tells Orde that he and his people prefer English policemen, for "native policemen are like small pox and criminal tribes put together."[15] He is made to elaborate on the theme of hate, vengeance, violence, and other gruesome matters. Kipling wants us to believe that the Jat is capable of posing as a model for Michelangelo, and invests him with the simple, honest virtues of a man of the soil. Yet he gives voice to feelings worthy of a savage. This is an irreconcilable incongruity.

The Jat's reference to the criminal tribes startles Pagett, thereby providing another opportunity for Orde to enter into a gruesome description. Orde takes a sadistic delight in working up dreadful pictures of cannibals to frighten the naïve Liberal member of Parliament. These criminal tribes according to Orde are: "Of great antiquity, a legacy from the past, the golden, glorious Aryan past of Max Müller, Birdwood and the rest of your spin drift philosophers."[16] With a stroke of his whip lash, a twist of satiric phrase, he dismisses the entire past culture of India as being worthless, leaving behind the legacy of criminal tribes. To increase this tortured vision and prove that there are only skulls and dead bones in India, Orde even digs up a skull, just by tapping the ground three times. India stands, therefore, amidst "the refuse of worked out cities and exhausted civilisations," among bones and cemeteries.[17] It is in this environment of hate, prejudice, and skeletons, of tired land and ignorant people that the Anglo-Indian must work. It is here that he has to civilize a race unwilling to be civilized. Hence Kipling repeats his chorus: the English deserve sympathy and understanding, but what the native deserves would, to use his own words, be another story. Kipling never told that story.

Pagett is also introduced to a young, educated Indian in the character of Dinanath. Dinanath is pictured as nervous, uncomfortable, speaking poor English, and superstitious. Dinanath is a second-year student at the mission college. He has come to request a promotion for his father. No Indian ever sent his son to an English

15 *Ibid.*, 364.
16 *Ibid.*, 365.
17 *Ibid.*, 385.

deputy commissioner to verbally request a promotion. Dinanath agrees that the congress is a great organization, complimenting Lord Ripon for his reforms.

Since Kipling never believed that education did or could do much good for the Indian people, he disliked seeing the Government and private agencies investing money in educational institutions for them:

> Good people in America, Scotland, and England, most of whom would never dream of collegiate education for their own sons, are pinching themselves to bestow it in pure waste on Indian youths.[18]

But later, when he criticizes the purely literary type of education given to the Indians, the reader is obliged to agree with him:

> Yet, as Lord Lansdowne pointed out the other day, the market is dangerously overstocked with graduates of our Universities who look for employment in the administration. An immense number are employed, but year by year the college mills grind out increasing lists of youths foredoomed to failure and disappointment, and meanwhile trade, manufactures, and the industrial arts are neglected and in fact regarded with contempt by our new literary mandarins *in posse*.[19]

This, of course, was not the fault of the people. They did not "neglect" and "regard with contempt" industries and manufacture for the very simple reason that there were none of these existing.

English educationists like Macaulay and Sir John Simon were responsible for charting the course of Indian education. The demands for scientific, technical, and vocational institutions were not adequately met because an increase in technically trained, industrial-minded Indians would spell disaster to Britain's home industry and manufacture. England, being mostly a manufacturing country, depended on raw material from abroad to keep her factories in operation. One example that might be pointed out is the cotton industry. Indian cotton was shipped to Lancashire to be manufactured into textiles. Britain could have started cotton factories in

[18] *Ibid.*, 370.
[19] *Ibid.*, 371.

India to give a fillip to Indian industry, but since she chose the other way, Gandhi launched a non-co-operation movement forbidding his countrymen to buy English-manufactured cotton. He started cottage industries, encouraged hand-spinning; and hand-woven cloth became a symbol of Indian protest against British industrial exploitation. Hence the charge that Indians looked upon industrial arts with contempt, seeking only literary pursuits, is a charge that, for lack of support, cannot be countenanced.

Pagett is interested in the possibility of bestowing electoral institutions on the people, a notion highly ridiculous to Kipling, who never believed in the sanctity of the ballot box. To impress Pagett with the idea that democracy could not work in India, he brings in an American, Dr. Eva McCreary Lathrop, for her opinion on the subject of native enfranchisement. Dr. McCreary, being an outsider, an American and therefore a strong believer in democratic ideals, is chosen because Kipling hopes, like the British propagandist he is, to convince Pagett of the stupidity of giving the vote to natives. Dr. McCreary asks:

> Wouldn't it be as much to the purpose to bestow point-lace collars on them? They need many things more urgently than votes. Why, it's like giving a bread-pill for a broken leg.[20]

To her, the trouble in India is not "in the least political," but something else. "It is an all-round entanglement of physical, social, and moral evils and corruptions, all more or less due to the unnatural treatment of women."[21]

Enfranchisement of the Indian could not be like "giving a bread-pill for a broken leg." It would give the Indian a voice in the management of the affairs of his own country, a sense of belonging, a feeling that he had a future in his country. The worst effect of alien rule is not so much physical exploitation as it is a moral and spiritual loss—the loss of individuality, the negation of all human freedom. The Indian had to solve his own problems. He would accept help, suggestion, and friendly co-operation with sympathy

[20] *Ibid.*, 380.
[21] Ibid., 380.

and understanding, but he would not accept dictation. Under the Imperial rule, where the Indian way of life was considered to be inferior and the English way the superior one, there could be no genuine co-operation. Education made the Indian aware of the backwardness of his country, particularly in science and technology. This awareness gave rise to political consciousness, which crystalized into organization of the Indian National Congress.

The official attitude toward the congress was based on the plea that the educated community—a "microscopic minority" as Lord Dufferin described it—had no right or claim to represent the views of India. The congress' reply to this argument embodies the sole justification of its representative character. It was ably summed up by Sir Ramesh Chandra Mitra in his speech as chairman of the reception committee of the congress held in Calcutta in 1896:

> The educated community represented the brain and conscience of the country, and were the legitimate spokesmen of the illiterate masses, the natural custodians of their interests. To hold otherwise would be to presuppose that a foreign administrator in the service of the Government knows more about the wants of the masses than their educated countrymen. It is true in all ages that those who think must govern those who toil; and could it be that the natural order of things be reversed in this unfortunate country.[22]

In his analysis of the Indian situation, Kipling betrays his ignorance on the one hand and his prejudice on the other. The past of India he did not care for; the present he could not understand. At the end of the story, "The Enlightenments of Pagett, M.P.," the reader sympathizes more with Pagett than with the Indians. Pagett, Groomsbride, and others like them were fooled, ridiculed, and attacked most ingloriously by officials like Orde and writers like Kipling. Thus when Pagett, after the interview with several Indians, says "India's a very curious place," Orde replies with the triumphant note of a warrior who has just won a battle, "Ah? You'll know all about it in three months. Come in to lunch."[23] "India's a curious place" might well be the title for Kipling's in-

[22] Mazumdar and Others, *An Advanced History of India*, III, 894.
[23] Kipling, "The Enlightenments of Pagett, M.P.," 386.

terpretation of India, for that is the picture of India emerging from most of his writings.

"The Head of the District" is written in the same mood of hate and prejudice as "The Enlightenments of Pagett, M.P." Here, again, is a defamation of the Bengali character, with a minute analysis of hatred in an Indian community resulting in mass violence. The story also ridicules the Liberal viceroy, Lord Ripon, who made it possible for an Indian to become the head of the district. There is grim irony in the very title of the tale, for the head of the district comes very close to losing his head in the violence that breaks out.

The story opens with a description of Orde, the deputy commissioner who acted as master of ceremonies in the show of hate and prejudice put up for the benefit of Pagett, M.P. Orde is about to die. He is expecting his wife, Polly, to come to see him. The Indus is in flood. Since it cannot be crossed, Polly has to wait until morning, when the waters recede to come over to his side. He may not last until morning. He thinks of his wife, of the district he has to leave, of his financial bankruptcy, and the tragic fact that he does not have even enough money to send his wife back to England. However, Tallantire, his assistant assures Orde that arrangements will be made to send Polly home, passing the hat around to collect a charity. Then follows one of Kipling's repetitious passages about the tragic plight of Anglo-Indians serving the queen while bearing the burden in India:

> It's not nice to think of sending round the hat; but, good Lord! how many men I lie here and remember that had to do it! Morten's dead—he was of my year. Shaughnessy is dead, and he had children; I remember he used to read us their school letters; what a bore we thought him! Evans is dead—Kot-Kumharsen killed him! Ricketts of Myndonie is dead—and I'm going too.[24]

We cannot accept that there existed such financial bankruptcy on the part of all of the deputy commissioners. There may have been mismanagement of funds, but a deputy commissioner, being an

---

24 "The Head of the District," *Life's Handicap*, 189.

important man, was well paid. There are records showing that the British Government made financial arrangements for Anglo-Indians to return to England at the end of a certain period.[25] Their allowances for family and housing were sufficient to enable them to lead a comfortable, if not luxurious, life. Kipling's complete blindness to these facts is unpardonable.

When Lord Ripon came out as the Indian viceroy in June, 1880, to implement a program of increased Indian participation in the country's administration, he had the full support of the British premier, Gladstone, for such an implementation. Lord Ripon was responsible for helping India along the road to self-government. The Indian historian Mazumdar comments:

> Lord Ripon's Resolution of May, 1882, aimed at the introduction of principles of self-government in municipal administration as in the case of rural Boards. He proposed that while the ultimate supervision . . . be in the hands of the Government, the actual municipal administration should be entrusted to the elected representatives of the people. . . . Thus Lord Ripon made a real beginning in the direction of local self-government in modern India . . . he sowed the seeds which ultimately germinated in a real development of local self-government.[26]

The very fact that the Indians liked Lord Ripon, considering him a great statesman, was sufficient to make the viceroy ridiculous in Kipling's eyes. He satirizes Ripon as "the Very Greatest of All the Viceroys." Lord Ripon's appointment of Indians to posts of responsibility, described as a "measure of political and popular education," alienated Kipling still further.[27]

It is against this political background of dislike for the viceroy and his reforms that the story, "The Head of the District," was conceived. When Orde dies, and the viceroy decides to appoint a Bengali, Mr. Grish Chunder De, to the vacancy, Kipling finds the very idea ridiculous:

> The very simplicity of the notion was its charm. What more easy

[25] Robert Carstairs, *The Little World of an Indian District Officer*, 220.
[26] Mazumdar and Others, *An Advanced History of India*, III, 860–61.
[27] *Ibid.*, 860.

to win a reputation for far seeing statesmanship, originality, and above all, deference to the desires of the people, than by appointing a child of the country to the rule of the country? Two hundred millions of the most loving and grateful folk under Her Majesty's dominion would laud the fact, and their praise would endure forever. Yet he was indifferent to praise or blame, as befitted the Very Greatest of All Viceroys. His administration was based upon principle, and the Principle must be enforced in season and out of season.[28]

All three persons in the story, the prime minister who encouraged Lord Ripon, the viceroy who encouraged the Bengali, and the Bengali who, in Kipling's opinion, was presumptuous enough to imagine that he could be the head of the district, are attacked bitterly. In the personality of Grish Chunder De, Kipling has brought to a climax all his detestation for the Bengali character.

Grish Chunder De, M.A., graduate of an Indian university, had traveled abroad and, "more English than the English," took Orde's place. De had won a seat in the civil service in open and fair competition with the "sons of the English"; he had even ruled a district in Bengal. Yet, with all these qualifications, since he was a member of an inferior race, no amount of training could make him equal to Orde, that fine specimen of Anglo-Saxon.

Another story of Kipling's shows how strongly he felt on the question of the superiority of race and its implied ability to command people. "His Chance in Life" is similar to the "Head of the District" in that someone other than an Anglo-Saxon is given an opportunity to take charge in a responsible situation. But De in "The Head of the District" fails, whereas Michele in "His Chance in Life" succeeds, the reason being a difference in racial quality, as we shall see.

Michele, a government telegraph signaler, was "very black, but he had his pride." He was part English, part Portuguese, and part native, hence "looked down on natives as only a man with seven eighths native blood in his veins can." It was in Tibasu, a little telegraph sub-office on the East coast of India, that his chance came. A riot breaks out in Tibasu, at the very first signs of which

28 "The Head of the District," 192.

Michele's assistant, a Bengali, "put on his cap and quietly dropped out of the window." When the town is in the grip of violence, the native police inspector, recognizing the "drop of white blood as far as it can be diluted," comes to take orders from Michele, the only representative of the English administration in that place.

While the Bengali flees, the one drop of white blood in Michele gives him presence of mind. He boldly walks in the streets, declaring to the elders of the town that "until the Assistant Collector came, the Telegraph Signaller was the Government of India in Tibasu." Peace settles on the disturbed city again. But when the genuine white man, the assistant collector, comes, Michele slips back into his native shell. Kipling admired Michele, for not only had he the drop of white blood, but what is more important, he recognized his position in the hierarchy of races. He is the "White Sahib" only when the real "White Sahib" is absent. With the arrival of the real "Sahib," he quickly withdraws to his inferior position. To Kipling, therefore, a drop of white blood in a man was much more important than all the training and education he could get. Hence, Grish Chunder De starts out with an initial disadvantage when he accepts appointment as head of the district.

In criticizing the Bengali, Kipling used the technique of making Indians themselves pass the verdict. He generally kept the Anglo-Indians out of the picture or had them take an indifferent attitude. This is to show that it is not so much the Anglo-Indians as the Indians themselves who despise the Bengali. This is clever propaganda, but very dangerous as a weapon inflaming racial hatred.

The action in "The Head of the District" takes place in the small district of Kot-Kumharsen. Kipling implies that what happens in this small district may happen all over India, if the British relinquish power to the natives. In the district, fierce rivalry existed between two men, Khoda Dad Khan and the Blind Mullah of Jagai, over the issue of tribal leadership. The rivalry was under control only because of the presence of the British. But with Orde's death, followed by De's appointment, violence breaks out, resulting in murder and looting. De, unlike Michele, cannot seize his chance in life, does not rise to the occasion, but flees in a cowardly manner, without even taking charge of the district,

> Thanking Gods entirely unknown to the most catholic of universities that he had not taken charge of the district, and could still —happy resource of a fertile race—fall sick.[29]

Not content with describing him as a coward, Kipling heaps on De even worse abuse through the mouths of the tribal leaders and their followers, who describe him contemptuously as "that black Bengali beast" and "an eater of fish from the South." Khoda Dad Khan is bitter when he says:

> He's a *kala admi*—a black man—unfit to run at the tail of a potter's donkey. All the peoples of the earth have harried Bengal. It is written. Thou knowest when we of the North wanted women or plunder whither went we? To Bengal—where else?[30]

All these are comments on the Bengali even before he enters the district. When he makes his appearance, the scene that follows reveals Kipling's intense dislike for any native occupying a position of importance in his own country:

> They the tribes people crowded to see him, pointing at him, and diversely comparing him to a gravid milch buffalo, or a broken down horse, as their limited range of metaphor prompted. They laughed at his police-guard, and wished to know how long the burly Sikhs were going to lead Bengali apes. They inquired whether he had brought his women with him, and advised him explicitly not to tamper with theirs. It remained for a wrinkled hag by the roadside to slap her lean breasts as he passed, crying, "I have suckled six that could have eaten six thousand of *him*. The Government shot them, and made this. That a king!" Whereat a blue turbaned huge boned plough-mender shouted, "Have hope, mother o' mine! He may yet go the way of thy wastrels." And the children, the little brown puff-balls, regarded curiously.[31]

[29] *Ibid.*, 205.
[30] *Ibid.*, 199.
[31] *Ibid.*, 204.

Against this hideous picture of the Bengali the English are presented as lawgivers, commanders, giving "sumptuous dinners and perhaps forbidden liquors; certainly with some wonderful tales and great good fellowship," to the tribal leaders, which makes Khoda Dad Khan say, "Orde Sahib was one prince and Tallantire another."[32] Even the Anglo-Indians do not seem to co-operate with the Bengali; thus De is forced to rely on his own resources. Like Michele, he telegraphs for help, but since he has no drop of white blood no one obeys him. He leaves the district in despair.

By his mere presence in the district, De has antagonized the various factions. Violence has erupted; Khoda Dad Khan's men have cut off the Blind Mullah of Jagai's head. To satisfy their fury they go in search of De, and find his brother riding alone. Mistaking him for the head of the district, they cut off his head.

> Slowly rolled to Tallantire's feet the crop-haired head of a spectacled Bengali gentleman, open eyed, open mouthed—the head of terror incarnate.[33]

Death then, brutal death, will be the reward for anyone trying to rule in place of the English. This is the implied message of the story.

After all this violence—men killed, property damaged, two heads at his feet—Tallantire assures the district that the government will send a *man*. Khoda Dad Khan says, "And by God, Sahib, may thou be that man."[34] This is propaganda at its worst. In the face of all this self-praise by the English, Kipling wrote in a poem, "The Puzzler," supposed to be an analysis of the English character: "The English—ah, the English—don't say anything at all."[35]

This portrayal of India is both unjust and out of focus with truth and reality. The Bengali was not detested outside his province, nor was he such a blundering, clumsy fool as Kipling makes him out to be. There may have been isolated cases of meanness and cowardice, but Kipling smears the entire community with vile abuse. He further takes the Bengali as representative of the educated In-

[32] *Ibid.*, 198.
[33] *Ibid.*, 213.
[34] *Ibid.*, 214.
[35] "The Puzzler," *Rudyard Kipling's Verse*, 533.

dian, thereby condemning the entire educated Indian community. Such incapacity to distinguish individuals from the group is indicative of Kipling's short-sighted and prejudiced nature.

The province of Bengal was one of the earliest to come under British rule. Before the Charter Act of 1853, the Bengal province consisted of Bengal, Bihar, Assam, Orissa, and the whole of the United provinces, with Delhi and a part of the Punjab thrown in.[36] Thus P. C. Ray is correct when he says, "At the beginning of the nineteenth century, Bengal practically meant India."[37] Bengal was also among the earliest to feel the impact of the West through English education. The East India Company and European missionary institutions set up a number of schools in and around the city of Calcutta. This probably accounts for the large number of pioneers in Indian thought and culture coming from Bengal.

Raja Ram Mohan Roy, already mentioned above, was a Bengali who co-operated with Lord William Bentinck, the Indian viceroy, in attacking social evils in the country. He was responsible for stopping the cruel custom of burning the widow along with her husband. Roy was also a great scholar, whose English prose style won the praise of Jeremy Bentham.[38] Then there was Pundit Ishwar Chandra Vidya Sagar, another Bengali and a great social reformer. Vivekananda, who interpreted the universality of Hinduism, winning the praise of William James; Rabindranath Tagore, the Nobel Prize winner for literature, whose poetry strengthened Yeats' belief in Indian mystic thought; Jagadish Chandra Bose, the Nobel Prize winner in biology for his demonstration of life among plants; P. C. Ray, the Nobel Prize winner in physics; Ashutosh Mukherjee, the famous educationist and vice-chancellor of the University of Calcutta, to name a few, were all Bengalis. The names of talented, gifted people from Bengal became numerous. They were and are respected in India for their genius and creative ability. These examples are sufficient to show that Kipling was completely wrong in his opinion of the Bengali.

[36] Prithwis Chandra Ray, *Life and Times of C. R. Das: The Story of Bengal's Self-Expression*, 1.
[37] *Ibid.*
[38] R. W. Frazer, *A Literary History of India*, 391.

Kipling dwelt on human skulls and wasted civilizations in "The Enlightenments of Pagett M.P."; on violence, race prejudice and two chopped-off heads in "The Head of the District." In "The Man Who Would be King" we are introduced to another chopped-off head, this time after it has been shriveled. The entire story has been written to prepare us for the climax of beholding the ghastly head of Daniel Dravot:

> He fumbled in the mass of rags around his bent waist; brought out a black horse hair bag embroidered with silver thread; and shook therefrom onto my table—the dried, withered head of Daniel Dravot! The morning sun that had long been paling the lamps struck the red beard and blind sunken eyes; struck, too, a heavy circlet of gold studded with raw turquoises, that Carnehan placed tenderly on the battered temples.[39]

In the story, "Dray Wara Yow Dee," written in the form of a Browningesque dramatic monologue, telling the vengeance of a man disappointed in love, we read of a similar mutilation:

> And she bowed her head, and I smote it off at the neck bone so that it leaped between my feet. Thereafter the rage of our people came upon me, and I hacked off the breasts, that the men of Little Malikand might know the crime, and cast the body into the water course that flows to the Kabul river.[40]

In "Namgay Doola" a cow's tail is cut off, setting the mood of violence. There is, again, a distasteful description in "Amir's Homily":

> A woman clamoured for divorce against her husband, who was bald, and the Amir, hearing both sides of the case, bade her pour curds over the bare scalp, and lick them off, that the hair might grow again, and she be contented.[41]

In "The Return of Imray" we read of the murder of Imray by one of his trusted servants, who concealed the body in the ceiling of the house where Strickland, the police officer, lived:

[39] "The Man Who Would Be King," *The Phantom Rickshaw and Other Stories*, 140.
[40] Kipling "Dray Wara Yow Dee," *In Black and White*, 8.
[41] "Amir's Homily," *ibid.*, 206.

94

I saw the ceiling cloth nearly in the centre of the room bag with a shape that was pressing it downwards towards the lighted lamp on the table. I snatched the lamp out of danger and stood back. Then the cloth ripped out from the walls, tore, split, swayed, and shot down upon the table something that I dared not look at. Strickland turned back the cloth for a moment, and looked. "It is Imray," he said; "and his throat is cut from ear to ear!"[42]

In the story, "In the House of Suddhoo," concerning black magic, Kipling again describes a gruesome, mutilated body as the climax of a weird ritual:

I looked at the basin, and saw, bobbing in the water the dried, shrivelled, black head of a native baby—open eyes, open mouth, and shaved scalp . . . . We had no time to say anything before it began to speak.[43]

Instances could be multiplied showing how Kipling dwelt on the strange, bizarre, and grotesque in picturing Indian life. "The Mark of the Beast," written in the pattern of Poe's horror tales, describes an Anglo-Indian assuming the features of a savage beast, as the result of a curse laid upon him by a Hindu leper priest. "The Strange Ride of Morrowbie Jukes" is another horror tale, wherein a Hindu is described eating crows in a most fearful manner. "My Own True Ghost Story," "The Phantom Rickshaw," "The Tomb of His Ancestors," and "The Gate of a Thousand Sorrows" all, for their plot and effect, rely upon the strange and peculiar in Indian life. They all have weird settings: the ghastly Dak Bungalow; the haunted road in Simla; the graveyard; and the opium den.

These stories about strange cults, of hidden occult powers, usually in the form of black magic, of brutal violence, of virile ghosts and haunted houses, belong in the category of "tall tales." The style of these stories "to put it baldly, is that of the gossip-column," they have come "by word of mouth."[44] Rumor, gossip—elements of casual conversation in a smoking room over a cup of coffee or a glass of beer—are the stuff of which these tales are made. The normal and the ordinary in Indian life seldom find expression

42 Kipling, "The Return of Imray," *Life's Handicap,* 320.
43 "In the House of Suddhoo," *Plain Tales from the Hills,* 153.
44 Carrington, "*The Life of Rudyard Kipling,* 69.

in his tales. Even in what might be considered normal stories like "William the Conqueror" and "Without Benefit of Clergy," famine and plague, respectively, provide the intensive backgrounds. The novel *Naulahka*, taking the form of an ill-written mystery story, relies on intrigue, motives of revenge, and attempts at poisoning. *Kim*, where everyday life in India finds a completely spontaneous expression, is the only exception.

Kipling's horror stories present no valid interpretation of India. The ghost stories could have taken place anywhere in the world; India has no monopoly on ghosts. Walter Morris Hart is of the opinion that Kipling's purpose in stories like "The Mark of the Beast" and "Return of Imray" was primarily to present a study of fear; to present states of human mind under the impact of black magic and other terrifying experiences.[45] It is difficult to accept this opinion, for if they were purely psychological tales, they have no abiding relevancy to the Indian scene. "The Mark of the Beast" need not have started in a Hindu temple, but could have taken place in a Jewish synagogue, a Moslem mosque, or a Burmese pagoda. Anglo-Indian Fleete could have behaved outrageously in any one of these locales. The tragic fate of Imray in "The Return of Imray" could have happened to any master with a superstitious servant. The phantom rickshaw could have been a phantom carriage or even an automobile. The Indian locale was not just a setting for his studies of the human mind under strain and stress; Kipling's primary purpose in these stories was to interpret India. He intended for his readers to reach the same conclusion as Pagett, M.P.— "India's a curious place." Neither the important work of Englishmen in linking India with the rest of the world, nor the hardy pioneering qualities that the Anglo-Saxon race possesses need be over-estimated. It is Kipling's lack of proportion in evaluating these that makes him guilty of gross distortion.

Kipling could write honestly about things that appealed to him without having to make any special effort to understand them. He liked the north of India and the Muslims who lived there. This admiration, however, was the result of a first impression and an

[45] *Kipling, the Story Writer*, 21–22.

accident of geography. He stated in his autobiography, "my life had lain among the Muslims, and a man leans one way or other according to his first service."[46] He writes of the north with fondness. In "Dray Wara Yow Dee," with all its fierce motive of revenge, there is a passage of rare beauty describing the northern countryside:

> Come back, with me to the North and be among men once more. Come back, . . . The bloom of the peach-orchards is upon all the valley, and here is only dust and a great stink. There is a pleasant wind among the mulberry trees, and the streams are bright with snowwater, and the caravans go up and the caravans go down, and a hundred fires sparkle in the gut of the Pass, and tent-peg answers hammer-nose, and pack horse squeals to pack horse across the drift smoke of the evening. Come back with me. Let us return to our own people! Come![47]

In similar terms, with almost the very same phrases, Kipling depicts the life of the northern frontiers in his poem "The Ballad of the King's Jest":

> In a turquoise twilight crisp and chill,
> A kafila camped at the foot of the hill.
> Then blue smoke-haze of the cooking rose,
> And tent-peg answered to hammer-nose;
> And the picketed ponies, shag and wild,
> Strained at their ropes as the feed was piled;
> And the bubbling camels beside the load
> Sprawled for a furlong adown the road;
> And the Persian pussy-cats, brought for sale,
> Spat at the dogs from the camel bale;
> And the tribesman bellowed to hasten the food;
> And the camp fires twinkled by Fort Jumrood;
> And there fled on the wings of the gathering dusk
> A savour of camels and carpets and musk,
> A murmur of voices, a reek of smoke,
> To tell us the trade of the Khyber woke.[48]

---

[46] *Something of Myself*, 75.
[47] Kipling, "Dray Wara Yow Dee," *In Black and White*, 5–6.
[48] "The Ballad of the King's Jest," *Rudyard Kipling's Verse*, 245.

In these scenic descriptions of the sights and sounds of northern India, Kipling reveals rare powers of observation. He can describe an Indian scene with vividness, but he cannot communicate with insight how an Indian thinks, or interpret his behavior in the light of his way of life. By judging the Indian from an Anglo-Saxon frame of reference, Kipling paints a tortured picture.

In a few rare cases, however, Kipling must be congratulated for showing an understanding of the native Indian mind. Three such cases can be cited: the northern Muslims, the tribal people, and the simple Indian women.

Kipling's liking for men of action made him admire the martial spirit of the Muslims. Like the British, they had been conquerors of India. The Muslims in the north, in the city of Lahore, the Punjab, and Sindh, were men of action who loved the great outdoors. They were hardy Pathans or courageous Afghans, with their own stern code of law and order. They co-operated with the British in a policy of live and let live, submitting to British rule but maintaining internal independence in their own tribal communities. Khoda Dad Khan, in "The Head of the District," kills the Blind Mullah of Jagai, but despite his ferocity, he prefers to be ruled by an English deputy commissioner like Orde or Tallantire. Mahbub Ali, the Pathan horse-merchant in *Kim*, wins Kipling's admiration for co-operating with the British in the "Great-Game." The Muslim servant, Muhammad Din, and his child are portrayed with sympathy and sensitivity, because they show faithfulness to the white master.

Among the Hindus, Kipling liked the Sikhs, a group of people who represent the militant aspect of Hinduism. They match the Muslims in their courage and love for physical action. Like the Muslims, they were a large Indian group joining the British forces. "Eyes of Asia" contains four letters supposedly written to relatives or friends at home in India by Sikh soldiers of the Indian army of Great Britain. On duty in France during the World War, they describe their experiences in that country. Kipling's admiration for these fighting men is evident in these letters.

In addition to the Muslims and the Sikhs, the tribal people receive understanding treatment at the hands of Kipling. "The Tomb of his Ancestors" is an exceedingly good story analyzing the tribal mind. The story, set in Central India, concerns the application of modern medical notions to a tribal people. The Chinn family occupied an Anglo-Indian community which had served India for generations. One of their achievements was bringing into the armed forces a unit of tribal people called "Wuddars," who "were irregulars, small, dark, and blackish, clothed in rifle green with black leather trimmings," and who dug up rats and ate them.[49] However strange their ways and customs, the fact that they belonged to the English regiment and were ready to fight for the British made them admirable in Kipling's eyes. They were a violent people, but "if handled discreetly grieved like children, and promised never to do it again."[50] They greeted Englishmen with respect:

> Chinn, flushed with triumph, was in the midst of it, . . . Wild folk came and pressed about his knees with offerings. He gave his flask to the elders of the village. They grew eloquent and wreathed him about with flowers. Gift and loans, not all seemly, were thrust upon him, and infernal music rolled and maddened round red fires, while singers sang songs of the ancient times, and danced peculiar dances.[51]

The Wuddars believed that one of the Chinns, Old Jan Chinn, who was buried in a grave in the region, occasionally rode out on a tiger. This legend is explained to the younger Chinn by another Anglo-Indian:

> Your reverend ancestor, my boy, according to the Bhils, has a tiger of his own—a saddle-tiger that he rides around the country, whenever he feels inclined. I don't call it decent in an ex-collector's ghost; but that is what the Southern Bhils believe. . . . It is supposed to be a clouded animal—not stripy, but blotchy, like a tortoise-shell tom-cat. No end of a brute it is, and a sure sign of war or pestilence or—or something.[52]

The legend grows stronger, leading to a belief among the tribal

[49] Kipling, "At the Tomb of His Ancestors," *In Black and White*, 131.
[50] *Ibid.*, 133.
[51] *Ibid.*, 138.
[52] *Ibid.*, 139.

folk that the younger Chinn is the reincarnated Older Chinn. They wish to see an end to these midnight wanderings of the ghostly tiger. The issue reaches a climax where the ghostly animal has to be shot or the Wuddars will neither join the army nor get vaccinated. By sheer coincidence, there is shot a tiger which to the natives is the animal in question, and they re-enlist in the army.

"The Tomb of His Ancestors" praises and flatters British capacity for handling dangerous situations. But more than that, the story is a fascinating study of the Indian tribal mind. Their strong belief in the reality of the unseen phenomena rather than the seen, the impact of their blind devotion bordering on superstition, and their maintenance of a rigid individualism are all part of the atmosphere of the story. Their customs, manners, way of life, fear of evil, and conception of a god of vengeance, find adequate treatment.

Kipling extends his admiration for the "simple natives" to include simple Indian women as well. In surprising contrast to his cynical portraits of the Anglo-Indian women, two portraits of Indian women, Lispeth in "Lispeth," and Ameera, in "Without Benefit of Clergy," are drawn with respect and seriousness. The two royal Indian queens in *Naulahka* come under a separate category, that of the women of high society in Indian life.

Lispeth is a hill girl converted to Christianity. Her family become Christians not because they need a better religion but, as Kipling tells us, for economic reasons:

> One year their maize failed, and two bears spent the night in their only opium poppy field just above the Sutlej Valley on the Kot-Garh side; so, next season they turned Christians, and brought their baby to the Mission to be baptized.[53]

But Lispeth falls in love with an Englishman, for "it takes a great deal of Christianity to wipe out uncivilized Eastern instincts, such as falling in love at first sight."[54] The man disappoints her, shattering her faith in Christianity. Her simple but startling question reveals both her innocence and the falseness of the Englishman and the missionary:

[53] "Lispeth," *Plain Tales from the Hills*, 3.
[54] *Ibid.*, 5.

"How can what you and he said be untrue?" asked Lispeth. "We said it as an excuse to keep you quiet, child," said the Chaplain's wife. "Then you have lied to me," said Lispeth, "you and he."[55]

Kipling consistently attacked the missionary in his attempt to convert the heathen. He preferred that these simple people be given material needs and comforts, "the cure of the body to the cure of the souls." For this reason Kipling admired Kate Sheriff, in the novel *Naulahka*. Kate goes to India not as a missionary to win souls, but on a medical mission to save lives, which is equally spiritual to Kipling.

"Without Benefit of Clergy" is one of Kipling's rare stories taking us into the interior of an Indian household and also into the mind of an Indian woman. The sixteen-year-old Ameera, being a Muslim, receives great attention and sympathetic presentation by Kipling. Bought by Holden from her mother, Ameera reveals the sensitive soul of a Muslim girl. The story has a romantic, sentimental atmosphere, intensified by the haunting song of Hardayal, which keeps returning in reminiscent strains. The romantic drama of Ameera and Holden is played out against the grim background of the Indian plague. Her spirit of self-sacrifice in refusing to leave her husband in spite of the approaching tragedy makes her a good example of the devoted Indian woman.

These two portraits of Indian women are brief, yet they give an indication, however slight, of Kipling's understanding of them. But for these rare moments of comprehension, his entire presentation of India would have reflected total misunderstanding and consequent misinterpretation.

[55] *Ibid.*, 6.

V

The Princely India: the Distorted Vision

*"Like everything else in a native
state—common talk, but difficult
to prove."*
—NAULAHKA.

NAULAHKA, A STORY OF WEST AND EAST, is Kipling's first attempt
at full-length treatment of an Indian theme. Written in collabora-
tion with the American writer, Wolcott Balestier, the implicit
purpose of the novel seems to be to contrast the ways of life in the
East and in the West. Within the framework of a melodramatic
plot concerning the experiences of two Americans, Tarvin and
Kate, in the backward Indian state of Rhatore, in Rajputana, India,
"the dead East" is contrasted with "the living West."[1]

East and West as presented in *Naulahka* are poles apart. The
values of the West, expressed in the dynamics of change and progress, are opposed to the values of the East, dead tradition, stagnation,
and superstition. The West in the form of Kate goes to change the
East, but fails, for

> It is not good for the Christian's health
> to hustle the Aryan brown,
> For the Christian riles and the Aryan smiles
> and he weareth the Christian down;
> And the end of the fight is a tomb stone
> white with the name of the late deceased,

[1] Rudyard Kipling, *Naulahka*, 121.

102

> And the epitaph drear: "A fool lies here who
> tried to hustle the East."[2]

The entire novel is devoted to an exposition of these views, and
to the familiar conclusion: "Oh, East is East, and West is West
and never the twain shall meet."[3]

Before we analyze this work seeking justification for these opinions, let us investigate the validity of the representations of "East"
and "West" in the novel.

The village of Topaz, Colorado, "a raw, untidy, lonely collection of ragged wooden buildings over a level plain" represents the
"West."[4] Topaz is provincial. Its citizens, represented by men like
Tarvin, consider the town their universe, with nothing beyond it.
Even the rest of the United States is another country to them,
except "in time of war."[5] There is Topaz' rivalry with its neighbor-
ing town of Rustler—not a healthy competition—for the citizens of
Topaz wish to see Rustler in the dust, "dead and buried," incapable
of rising again. Situated in the western wilderness, isolated from the
rest of the country and the world, seething with narrow pride,
Topaz is representative neither of the United States nor of the
Western world.

In the novel, Kipling implies that Topaz is not typical of the
entire United States, but only of a section of the American west.
But with Rhatore, which is meant to symbolize the "East" Kipling
attempts no such clarification. Except for the first five chapters,
the novel has Rhatore as its setting. No other part of India or of the
"East" ever enters the novel. Kate's brief stay is confined to
Rhatore, yet she is described as spending time in the "East." The
lazy, ill-equipped stationmaster, who has never been outside the
city limits of Rhatore, is described as "the East," becoming the
personification of the Orient. Tarvin spends a few days in Rhatore,
and promptly learns the secret of the "East," "never to be sur-

[2] *Ibid.,* 63.

[3] Rudyard Kipling, "The Ballad of East and West," *Rudyard Kipling's Verse,*
233.

[4] Kipling, *Naulahka,* 51.

[5] *Ibid.,* 33.

prised at anything."[6] Rhatore, therefore, becomes a microcosm of the "dead East."

By its very existence as a native state, Rhatore has lost its capacity to represent all of the East or India. The native states under the British constituted "Princely India." Occupying two-fifths of India, they had a strange relationship to the rest of the country. Independent, aristocratic, with a long and venerable ancestry, the Indian Prince had come to look upon the state as his own. The best of princes became benevolent despots, the worst, tyrants. They accepted, however, the protection of the British Crown, subscribing to the principle of paramountcy by which Great Britain controlled the foreign affairs of each of the states, with the right to interfere in a state's domestic affairs in event of any maladministration or gross injustice by its rulers. In India, yet not a part of it, under the British, yet foreign, their paradoxical position was ably summed up by Sirdar Panikkar, an authority on Indian native states:

> Though they vary in size, population, revenue, and the extent of the rights they enjoy, there is one fact which is common to them, that is, their territory is not British and their people are not subjects of the British Crown. British Indian Courts have no jurisdiction inside even the smallest States and the laws passed by the Indian Legislature do not, except in certain cases, in relation to British subjects, extend to the States. Legally, they are foreign territory.[7]

These native states, totaling more than five hundred, varied in size and administration. On the one hand, there were states like Hyderabad, Mysore, Travancore, and Kashmir, veritable countries in size. On the other, there were states consisting of only a few acres, with a population of less than fifty, like the state of Bilbari, which had a population of twenty-seven, an area of 1.65 square miles, with a revenue of eighty rupees ($16.00), remnants from a remote past.[8]

The native states retained much of the picturesqueness, pag-

---

[6] *Ibid.*, 93.

[7] *An Introduction to the Study of the Relations of Indian States with the Government of India*, 32.

[8] John Gunther, *Inside Asia*, 468.

eantry, and color of medieval India. Here Maharajas held glittering courts and sponsored costly festivities, tiger hunting, and entertainments on a lavish scale for visitors. In the larger and more progressive states, like Mysore and Baroda, these festivities reflected the ancient culture of the people. Myth and legend, epic and saga, music and dancing, all combined to make these festivities colorful, keeping a vital link with the past and providing relief from the monotony of everyday life.

This festive spirit, with both the ruler and the people taking part, was not common to all native states. There were states, small and backward, whose Maharajas spent most of their time out of residence. Imbibing the superficialities of Western culture, they wasted time and energy as playboys on the Riviera, moving in the elegance of London, Paris and Vienna. This type of gay, carefree, glittering, and reckless life of the native Indian prince has provoked severe criticism from a member of their own clan. Princess Brinda, of the tiny state of Kapurthala, in her autobiography, *Maharanee*, commmented on the hollowness of the princes, pursuing physical pleasure while their subjects and the state were falling into dejection and decay. They were, to borrow an apt description from John Gunther, "anachronistic pools of absolutism in the modern world," living off the fat of the land.[9]

Seen against this bewildering variety existing among the native states, Rhatore cannot even be considered representative of all the native states. It represents, at best, a small group of backward Rajputana states in Central India. *Naulahka* can be considered only as a novel of local color.

In describing this novel, *A Tale of West and East*, Kipling again revealed his tendency to make broad, sweeping generalizations. He could not resist frequently using terms like "East," "West," and the "Orient," which he did not attempt to define. These terms were catchy, glib, and romantic, counter-words that captured the journalist in Kipling. Furthermore, they provided the economy of expression he was seeking in his writings. But brevity often resulted in imprecision, for Kipling applied these comprehensive

[9] *Ibid.*, 464.

terms in a limited sense, the part for the whole, thereby revealing
his limitations in assessing the problem. *Naulahka* has an imposing
sub-title, *A Tale of West and East*, but the *West* is a small town in
the U.S.A., and the *East*, a backward state in India.

Take, for example, that oft-quoted and well-known "The Ballad
of East and West," where the theme of East-West relations is
worked out in an incident of the Indian frontier. Structurally, the
ballad approaches perfection. In its galloping rhythm, vivid word
pictures, and imagery evoking the spirit of the restless Indian frontier, it favorably stands comparison with one of Scott's best ballads,
"Lochinvar." But, in its analysis of the central theme of East-West
meeting, the ballad is an intellectual failure.

Kamal, a border outlaw, is the representative of the "East." His
stealing the Colonel's favorite mare sets off the action. The dangerous pursuit by the Colonel's son (who, incidentally, represents
the "West"), trying to recapture the mare, only ends in Kamal's
cornering him. The Colonel's son reminds his captor that if he
should be killed, an entire troop of English soldiers would ravage
the border town. He demands his mare, so that he can find his
way back. These bold words appeal to the hardy Kamal, who is
soon converted, gives himself up, and more than that, orders his
young son to join the British army. His parting words to his son are:

> "Now here is thy master," Kamal said,
>   "who leads a troop of the Guides,
> And thou must ride at his left side as
>   shield on shoulder rides.
> 'Till Death or I cut loose the tie, at
>   camp and board and bed,
> Thy life is his—thy fate it is to guard
>   him with thy head.
> So thou must eat the White Queen's
>   meat, and all her foes are thine,
> And thou must harry thy father's hold
>   for the peace of the Border-line,
> And thou must make a trooper tough
>   and hack thy way to power—

Belike they will raise thee to Ressaldar
when I am hanged in Peshawur."[10]

The poem concludes with the refrain that East and West have met in the sons of Kamal and the Colonel.

This ballad is as unbelievable as picturing the leader of the Mau Mau movement surrendering arms to Queen Elizabeth II and taking up position as her personal bodyguard. The ballad is an attempt to make the point that in recognition of mutual strength, two people can meet on common ground, even though they represent East and West. In the first place, there is not much "strength" in the ballad. All that Kamal does is run away with the Colonel's mare. All that the Colonel's son does is play upon the fear of revenge when his life is in danger. Kamal, an outlaw, an uncompromising opponent of British rule, is converted by the brave words of the Colonel's son. There is not much bravery in hiding behind the fear of revenge. Kamal's quick conversion leads the reader to believe that he was not very strong after all. His son is a passive character who merely obeys his father's command. Therefore, the ballad celebrates no heroic incident.

The moment Kamal sends his son to the British army to serve "The White Queen," East and West have met, in Kipling's view. By no stretch of imagination can the outlaws of the Indian frontier represent "the East." Equally, no single British regiment can stand for the West. It is an Indian border ballad, full of local color, and merely records an incident in the process of subjugating the Indian frontiersmen to British rule. Kipling's use of "East" and "West" suffers from limited application.

Kipling's knowledge of the Indian states was both limited and superficial. A brief visit to the central Indian native states in November, 1887, as part of a reporting assignment for the *Pioneer*, constituted all of his personal experience with "Princely India." His reports, first published in the *Pioneer*, were later collected into a volume, *The Letters of Marque*.

Written to specification and to meet a deadline, *The Letters of Marque* bears the imprint of hack reporting. They are the notes

[10] Kipling, "The Ballad of East and West," 236.

of a tourist, full of hasty impressions, sketchy descriptions, and monotonous repetition. All the central Indian Rajputana states suffer from the heat and dust of their environment. Their medieval architecture is full of forts, subterranean passages, moats for protection from the enemy, and dingy court halls. There is so much repetitious description of these features that the reader gets no clear picture of any single state. These Rajput states, tracing their origins to remote history, had surrounded themselves with myths, legends, epics, and sagas. They celebrated heroism, valor, and incidents from traditional history emphasizing a moral principle or strength of character. In referring to these tales Kipling assumed a tone of cynicism and indifference. Customs and manners of the Rajput heroic age were to him curiosities with neither meaning nor purpose. Since he covered these states hastily and, therefore, superficially, he was unable to enter into the lives of the people, which might have helped him gain a deeper and richer insight.

Kipling himself was conscious of the evanescent quality of *The Letters of Marque*. He was compelled to publish them because of "the enterprise of various publishers who, not content with disinterring old newspaper work . . . have seen fit to embellish it with additions and interpolations."[11]

In contrast to *The Letters of Marque* stands E. M. Forster's *The Hill of Devi*, a collection of letters revealing life and its problems in an Indian state. Forster's knowledge of the Indian state of Dewas Senior is extensive. He was the ruler's private secretary and, more than that, was in touch with the inner workings of the state over a period of thirty years.[12] As a result of this intimate association, Forster is able to present a much more valid picture of the native Indian state than Kipling. In describing the native state—"the oddest corner of the world outside Alice in Wonderland"—Forster makes an honest attempt to understand the traditions and problems confronting it. He not only describes places and incidents but also reveals an astonishing insight into them. This insight appears in the description of the Hindu festival of "Gokulashtami." The fun and

---

[11] Kipling, *From Sea to Sea*, I, Preface.
[12] E. M. Forster, *The Hill of Devi*, 7.

fellowship of the festival are minutely explained, but at the same time Forster shows how significantly myth and legend affect the life of the simple people of the state. He also presents a very penetrating study of that much maligned character, the Maharaja, which we shall compare to Kipling's portrait of the Maharaja in *Naulahka*.

The Letters of Marque became the source book for *Naulahka*. Descriptive passages, incidents and phrases were lifted in their entirety from the former into the latter. Tarvin's first audience with the Maharaja of Rhatore parallels the description of the Englishman's meeting with the Maharaja of Jodhpur in *The Letters*.[13] The elaborate description of the dead city of Gunnaur with the "Gow-Mukh" (The Cow's Mouth) to which Tarvin journeys in search of the jewel, Naulahka, is a close approximation of the dead city of Amber.[14] Kipling used this description again in the story of "The King's Ankus" in *The Second Jungle Book*, to depict the dead city with the buried treasure. Kate's first sight of the dilapidated, ill-equipped Rhatore State Dispensary, with crowds of sick people, including those who suffered from "loin-bite," is an exact replica of the state dispensary of Boondi in *The Letters*.[15] The statement by the Boondi doctor, "All folk, even little children, eat opium here,"[16] is echoed by the Rhatore doctor, Dhunpat Rai, to Kate, "All Rajputs eat opium."[17] The idea for the character of Kate herself came from the character of the Scotch Presbyterian minister in Udaipur. The minister was in the native state both as a preacher and a doctor. Like Kate, he had faith that "sends a man into the wilderness."[18] The Jodhpur prince, the Maharaja of Kunwara, "the apple of the Maharaja's eye, and one of the quaintest little bodies that ever set an Englishman disrespectfully laughing," was the inspiration for the Maharaja Kunwara in *Naulahka*.[19]

There is nothing objectionable in a writer's making free use of

13 Kipling, *From Sea to Sea*, I, 124–25.
14 *Ibid.*, 18, 115.
15 *Ibid.*, 151.
16 *Ibid.*, 152.
17 *Naulahka*, 147.
18 Kipling, *From Sea to Sea*, I, 60.
19 *Ibid.*, 125.

his journals or earlier writings as source material for later work. But in the present case, Kipling does not effect a useful transformation of the earlier *Letters* into the later novel. By "dumping" in all the evil, intrigue, and desolateness that ever existed in all of the central Indian states to make Rhatore an "evil land, close to the gates of Hell,"[20] Kipling reveals his lack of proportion in handling the theme of native Indian states. *Naulahka* becomes a mere scissors and paste production, without depth of feeling or insight into life.

As a result of his limited experience, Kipling presents a one-sided view of the situation. In the story "The Miracle of Puran Bhagat," however, there is a brief reference to a progressive Indian native state tucked up "somewhere in the north-western part of the country."[21] This state makes great strides in moral and material progress as a result of its implicit belief in the theory that "what was good for the Englishman must be twice as good for the Asiatic."[22] But here the state is only incidental to the story, a mere backdrop for the personality of Puran Bhagat. With this possible exception, there is no favorable reference to the Indian states throughout the range of Kipling's writings. Kipling looked upon the native states as "... dark places of the earth, full of unimaginable cruelty, touching the Railway and the Telegraph on one side, and on the other, the days of Harun-al-Raschid."[23]

Repeatedly, he stamps native states with "unimaginable cruelty." Carnehan, in "The Man Who Would Be King," describes Degumber state, where the Rajah fills his father's widow with red pepper and swings her to death as she hangs from a beam.[24] In *Kim*, the five native states are involved in intrigue and conspiracy, while the smaller hill rajahs carry on a "mysterious slave traffic" in women.[25] "A Legend of the Foreign Office" records with biting scorn the whims and fancies of Rustum Beg of Kolazai, "a slightly

[20] Kipling, *Naulahka*, 114.
[21] Kipling, "The Miracle of Puran Bhagat," *The Second Jungle Book*, 175.
[22] *Ibid.*, 176.
[23] "The Man Who Would Be King," *The Phantom Rickshaw and Other Stories*, 90.
[24] *Ibid.*, 43–44.
[25] Rudyard Kipling, *Kim*, 112.

backward Indian state," who showers benefits on his people one day and tyrannizes them the next. Human sacrifice to sacred crocodiles, attempts at poisoning, intrigue in the palace, child marriage, are some of the features of life in Rhatore in *Naulahka*. This preoccupation with incidents that are sensational, shocking, or full of suspense reveals Kipling's keen desire to tell an effective story. In concentrating on the cruel, mysterious, and strange, Kipling accepted the native states as "created by Providence in order to supply picturesque scenery, tigers and tall writing."[26] It was against this background and in this mood that *Naulahka* was written.

Rhatore and Topaz, Colorado, are strikingly similar in appearance. Yet, they differ in spirit, for Topaz, with all its seeming "untidy and raw" atmosphere, possesses the "git and go" of the American spirit. This is revealed in the personality of Tarvin, the practical, down-to-earth American. He possesses drive, force, and the restless desire of Western man to build, to sell, and to amass fortunes. All these qualities are exhibited in his passionate desire to make his city a metropolis of the west.

The Three C's—The California, Colorado Central Railroad— is the only thing that could successfully bring about this transformation. Tarvin seeks to realize his dream by inviting the president of the Three C's to Topaz, arranging a tour of the town, speaking persuasively to him, and carefully elaborating on the unlimited possibilities of commercial expansion in Topaz—in short, by using all the techniques of a high-pressure salesman.

Behind the President of the Three C's is his wife, Mrs. Mutrie, upholding the favorite Kipling maxim, "there is a woman at the back of everything." Like Cornelia Agrippina who "controlled a humble husband, who in turn controlled a Department," Mrs. Mutrie controlled her husband, the President of the Three C's, with supreme confidence that "I guess what I say to Jim goes."[27] Tarvin exploits her weakness for jewels, promising the fabulous "Naulahka" from India in return for her assistance in bringing the Three C's to Topaz. The scheme is repulsive to Tarvin because it places the destiny of

---

26 The Man Who Would Be King," 90.
27 Kipling, *Naulahka*, 61.

a civilized Christian town like Topaz in the hands of the uncivilized heathens of Rhatore. His passion for progress, however, overcomes this slight disturbance of conscience.

In some respects, Rhatore, stands in painfully sharp contrast to Topaz. Its desolate railroad junction, which is the first landmark seen by an arriving visitor, is a "final, intended, absolute," indication of the very spirit of the state.[28] "No new railroad could help Rawut Junction. It had no ambition. It belonged to the Government."[29] The bullock-cart drive that Tarvin takes is characteristic of the slow, lifeless, drowsy movement of Rhatore. The very atmosphere of the town is benumbing. It retards progress, decreases enthusiasm, and gives rise to futility and despair. The group of aggressive, high-pressure salesmen, whom Tarvin finds waiting on the palace porch to collect dues from the Maharaja, have learned to accept the slow movement of life in Rhatore. Estes, the American missionary from Bangor, Maine, had come with high hopes and strenuous endeavors, but since everyone else grew idle in the state, he also had become a victim of apathy.

Man and nature have conspired to make Rhatore a human jungle. Its court is full of intrigue, gossip and scandal, the inevitable accessories of a small out-of-the-way native state. E. M. Forster comments on such an atmosphere in his book, *The Hill of Devi*. Reviewing the situation in the State of Dewas, Senior, he writes:

> There was endless gossip, there were exhausting squabbles, particularly between his mother and aunt, there were all the grievances of the zenana over jewelry and precedence, connecting with the grievances of males outside, there were marriage connections with other courts, fertile in other grievances and, hidden in this vast domestic hotbed, there was always the possibility of poison. I know of no case at Dewas either of poisoning or of attempted poisoning. But I can recall no less than three poison scares.[30]

In Rhatore, poverty breeds ignorance, and ignorance gives rise to superstition, which in turn is exploited by fanatical pseudo-holy

[28] *Ibid.*, 64.
[29] *Ibid.*
[30] *The Hill of Devi*, 61.

men. Blind tradition puts up an obstinate fight against modern progress. Therefore, Rhatore stagnates with a dead past, a desolate present, and a bleak future. There is faithful attention to detail in the physical descriptions of the state. The "narrow sand-choked streets"; the dismal, ill-lighted post office, a mockery of modern progress; relics of ruined palaces and crumbling forts; the Hindu temple of the Bull facing the ugly statue of a forgotten British officer; are all described with photographic realism. Equally graphic is the picture of the dead city of Gunnaur with the Cow's Mouth, deep underground passages, coiled-up snakes, scattered skulls and slimy alligators. There is also a vivid report of the desert landscape:

> At dawn the rocks glittered like diamonds, and at noon day the sands of the rivers troubled his eyes with a million flashing sparks. At even tide a cold, dry wind would spring up, and the hills lying along the horizon took a hundred colours under the light of the sunset. Then Tarvin realised the meaning of "the glorious East," for the hills were turned to heaps of ruby and amethyst, while between them the mists in the valleys were opal.[31]

In all this, Kipling is the dutiful and diligent reporter. But in being a reporter, Kipling loses track of insight into the Indian character, *Naulahka* can reconstruct for the reader the physical atmosphere of a backward Indian state, but not its mind and spirit. An analysis of native character as portrayed in *Naulahka* will reveal Kipling's lack of understanding of this aspect of Indian life.

The Maharaja of Rhatore is the most important Indian character in the novel. Analysis of his personality may serve as the touchstone for evaluating Kipling's capacity to portray the native Indian state. But Kipling is exceedingly satiric and cynical in his delineation of the Maharaja, so that instead of a character portrayal, we have a caricature.

In Kipling's hands the Maharaja becomes repulsive. Addicted to opium, maintaining a harem, negligent in his management of everyday activities, submissive to the wily machinations of his gypsy queen, Sitabhai, the Maharaja is vain, lazy, and selfish. He

---

[31] Kipling, *Naulahka*, 72.

owns the fabulous jewel, "Naulahka," yet his state is poverty-stricken. He is enraged by the constant interference of the British Resident, Colonel Nolan, yet lacks the courage to stand up to him. He controls enormous man power, but hasn't the knowledge necessary to mobilize it for useful work. He is aware of evil and intrigue in the court but is indifferent to it. Pig hunting, playing "pachisi" (Indian Chess), and watching Tarvin shoot a coin in the air constitute his entertainment. Childishly, he shows his eagerness to "hear the earth shake and see the rocks fly" when Tarvin blows up the dam over the river Amet.

This portrait of the Maharaja leaves the reader dissatisfied. Here is an enumeration of his vices and eccentricities, but no insight into his mind. The study of the Indian Maharaja would have gained in stature and purpose if Kipling, instead of merely being the diligent reporter of life as observed, had attempted to see beneath the surface. What were the forces that shaped the mind of a Maharaja? Why was he a strange combination of the simple and the complex? True, the Indian Maharaja lived in a world of crumbling forts and dark palaces, but what was his emotional world, his spiritual conflicts, his complex problems of state and self? These questions find no answer in the novel. In fact, Kipling never recognized the existence of such questions, for he was a reporter pure and simple, displaying the superficialities of Indian life as seen in a backward native state.

The Indian native Prince lived between two worlds, the old world of regal authority, tradition, and medieval splendor that was dying out, and the new world of modern ideas, state legislatures and canals creeping in. His problem was to achieve a synthesis of the two. Some succeeded, others escaped, a few failed. And the world always took note of these failures. E. M. Forster, in *Hill of Devi*, quotes the obituary notice of the Maharaja of the State of Dewas, Senior, that appeared in the London *Times*, and comments forcefully on the complete lack of understanding by the Western world of the real personality of the Indian Maharaja, the man behind the external trappings of a feudal order. This passage from Forster, though long, is quoted in its entirety, because it indicates by implication the type of reporting upon which Kipling based his entire study of the personality of the Indian ruler:

The *Times* of London duly carried an obituary notice of him. It is a model of ungenerosity and prim indignation and I read it with rage. The rage has subsided, for after all what else could the *Times* carry? Here was an Indian Ruler who had not been a success, who had maladministered his state and got into debt and given the Government of India trouble, who had not even been frank when invited by British officials to be so. "He came of an ancient and renowned dynasty, and in the early years of his rule gave some promise of doing well, but an ungovernable temper and self-indulgence led to serious deterioration." The progress of the deterioration is traced; his marriage and its failure, the departure of the Kolhapur Princess, his feud with her house, his troubles with his son are all described, not from his point of view, but the point of view of his enemies; his appeal to Ramsay MacDonald and his penitential fasts are sneered at. There is not one hint that he was lovable and brilliant and witty and charming, and (more exasperating still) not one hint that he was complex. He will go down to history as a failure. That is the sort of thing that does go down to history.[32]

Kipling's Maharaja of Rhatore in *Naulahka* is a study in failure. Seen against the commentary by Forster, Kipling's superficialities are self-evident. If the reader is outraged at the ridiculous portrait of the Maharaja, he can only find consolation by concluding, what else could Kipling portray?

The other Indian characters in *Naulahka* are equally far-removed from the realities of Indian court life. The queen is supposed to embody the silent, suffering, passive qualities of ideal Indian women. But, in creating her personality to these specifications, Kipling has not only repeated his offense of superficiality but also portrayed an unimpressive and unrealistic character.

The portrait of the Indian queen in *Naulahka* must be examined in the light of a queen's position in an Indian court. Maharajas took many wives, and the zenana was an integral part of the royal household, where a carefully defined hierarchy existed. The first wife

---

[32] *The Hill of Devi*, 265.

of the Maharaja, the chief queen, always enjoyed a position of dignity and respect, even if she lost favor with her royal master. If she were the mother of the heir-apparent, regardless of the way the Maharaja treated her, she attained almost a religious sanctity. When the chief queen lost favor with the Maharaja she often went into retirement, spending her time in meditation or listening to readings from the sacred scriptures, from which she drew spiritual consolation and strength for her life of quiet resignation. In *Naulahka*, Kipling attempts to present such a chief queen, exemplary, ideal, and noble, one who has fallen only because of her innocence in courtly intrigue. While the attempt deserves praise, the portrait itself is not convincing because of his limited knowledge of the mind and heart of an Indian queen.

The queen in *Naulahka* describes herself as a "widow" in spite of the fact that her husband, the Maharaja, is still alive. To her, he is dead, for he is under the evil influence of the youthful gypsy queen, Sitabhai, who is adept in the art of holding men in her power. So the queen recedes into the background, into darkness, and lives in self-imposed solitude, "a stranger among stranger people."

Kipling wanted his readers to be impressed with the Oriental wisdom, philosophic mind, and calm resignation of the queen. Yet he did not really create a character deserving of admiration. The interview between Kate and the queen serves to bring out both Kipling's intended purpose and his weakness in the execution of it. Kate is disappointed. Her hospital has been deserted and her good work ignored since a fanatical holy man has convinced the people of Rhatore that Kate is a sorceress employing evil forces in the form of pills and pastes to destroy them. She has an audience with the chief queen, accompanying Prince Kunwara, whom she has protected from poisoning at the hands of Sitabhai. In this meeting between the two women, Kipling intends to present "Eastern Wisdom," as seen in the chief queen, and "Western Knowledge" as found in Kate.

The chief queen, though ignorant of modern ways, possesses rich experience. Personal suffering and old age have brought her a mellow and balanced outlook on life. Kate, on the other hand, is young and idealistic, but full of the technical knowledge of medical treatment for the sick and wounded. She lacks, however, the maturity of the chief queen. The chief queen is not oblivious to the outstanding quality of service which Kate has demonstrated in her devotion to the people of Rhatore, but she attempts to point out a weakness, that Kate is unmarried and therefore has not experienced the joy and suffering of motherhood. She questions Kate's ability to serve and save life:

> Little sister, how couldst thou understand life that hast never given it? Hast thou ever felt the tug of the child at the breast? . . . There was no child in thy arms. The mother look was not in thy eyes. By what magic, then, wouldst thou speak to women? There was a charm among the drugs, they said, and their children would be misshapen. What didst thou know of the springs of life and death to teach them otherwise?[33]

In the speech of the chief queen Kipling is trying to show the great emphasis that Indian women place on the value of marriage, family, and children. This noble intention is commendable, but has not found effective expression, since his knowledge of Indian women was very limited.

Therefore, the interview between Kate and the queen leaves the unimpressive picture of a queen who doles out "Eastern Wisdom" in a capsule: "Be a mother and everything will be right." The queen's suggestion is not in harmony with the rest of the story. Kate fails, not because she has no child of her own, but as a result of the domination of Indian women by their husbands.

> Kate called on the women by name, beseeching them to stay, reasoning, arguing, expostulating. But to no purpose. Many of them were in tears; but the answer from all was the same. They were sorry, but they were only poor women, and they feared the wrath of their husbands.[34]

The queen is mistaken in her evaluation of Kate's influence on the Indian women. Kipling wants the queen's interpretation to be valid,

[33] Kipling, *Naulahka*, 342–343.
[34] *Ibid.*, 321.

for soon after talking with her, Kate leaves the state of Rhatore and begins to think of marriage. All this reveals the hastily contrived plot of the novel.

Kipling could have made the queen more impressive by making her interview with Kate more meaningful. Essentially, what Kate lacks is not marriage and a child, but the ability to be patient, and understanding, and get into the tempo of Indian life rather than walk about like an "angel of the Lord" with a stern, puritanical face. Kate needed tact. She was facing a new set of ideas in Rhatore, and she needed moral support not only from her own people but also from someone native to the state. The queen, whom Kipling wants to be patient and strong as a result of her suffering, could have given Kate this support. The Indian woman admires service for its own sake. The Indian household accepts the fact that an individual should do his work devotedly and selflessly, with no immediate expectation of reward, leaving the final judgment to Providence. Therefore, when the queen ignores Kate's unselfish work and challenges her qualifications, Kipling is not only presenting a distorted picture of the queen, but shattering the very foundation on which he set out to build her character.

The portrait of the queen, like those of the other characters in the novel, has been contrived from the outside. Kipling was unable to render the thoughts and actions of a queen. In attempting to make her profound by trite statements, he has made her character a masterpiece of noble triviality.

In the portrayal of the gypsy queen, Sitabhai, Kipling set out to present a contrast to the chief queen. The Maharaja is drab and monotonous, the chief queen passive and shallow, Prince Kunwara sickly and pale; but in Sitabhai Kipling hopes to capture the exoticism and romanticism of India. The Indian gypsy, in colorful dress, fancy trinkets, and primitive arrogance, wandering from place to place, singing strange ballads of love and revenge, professing to read palms and foretell the future, is an exciting character. Kipling is not wrong in selecting the gypsy to enhance the romantic atmosphere of the novel. It is in his treatment of her that he has failed once again. Sitabhai is presented as the *femme fatale* of the novel. She has a dark past, full of cunning plots, selfish interests, and bloody violence. Having risen from a common street gypsy to the status of a queen, she has spread her tentacles octopus-like, both within the palace and outside. She has lured the Maharaja away from his rightful wife; disrupted the economy of the state by refusing to allow a canal to run through her orange garden; attempted to poison the prince, who is an obstacle in the way of her own son becoming a ruler; and she has even tried to be unfaithful to the Maharaja in her midnight rendezvous with Tarvin.

All these traits, plus her thirst for revenge, could make a masterful character of the gypsy Sitabhai. But as Kipling handles it, there is no growth in the character. The reader meets her for the first time in the desert with Tarvin, and there is an enumeration of her evil intentions and wicked deeds in the past. This abrupt cataloging makes the portrait crowded, too sudden, too contrived; hence when Tarvin is impressed after hearing of the gypsy's career, the reader fails to share his enthusiasm.

Sitabhai, it must be understood, is an Indian gypsy. As such, for all her wild, primitive code she is still part of the world of the Indian woman. But there seems to be nothing Indian about her except her name. She is reminiscent of the bold, bad women in tales of the American wild west. She is found riding horseback in the desert, suspicious, aware of danger but always planning to outwit the enemy, quick to pull the trigger and constantly swearing. The following incident is an example of the tempo of the wild west found in the portrait of Sitabhai. Tarvin snatches the fabulous "Naulahka" from her and attempts to ride away, when the struggle between the two begins:

> He bent to make sure of his girth. The Queen, standing behind her horse, waited an instant to mount. "Good-bye, Tarvin Sahib; and remember the gypsy," she said, flinging her arm out over the horse's withers. "Heh!" A flicker of light passed his eye. The jade handle of the Queen's knife quivered in the saddle-flap half an inch above his right shoulder. His horse plunged forward at the Queen's stallion, with a snort of pain.

"Kill him, Juggut Singh!" gasped the Queen, pointing to Tarvin, as the eunuch scrambled into his saddle. "Kill him!"

Tarvin caught her tender wrist in his fast grip. "Easy there, girl! Easy!" She returned his gaze, baffled. "Let me put you up," he said.

He put his arms about her and swung her onto the saddle.

"Now give us a kiss," he said, as she looked down at him.

She stooped. "No, you don't! Give me your hands." He prisoned both wrists, and kissed her full upon the mouth. Then he smote the horse resoundingly upon the flank, and the animal blundered down the path and leaped out into the plain.

He watched the Queen and Juggut Singh disappear in a cloud of dust and flying stones, and turned with a deep sigh of relief to the lake.[35]

This passage is like one of the shallow scenes that Hollywood presents to recall the so-called glory of the wild west when "men were men and women were women and glad of it."

Earlier, Sitabhai is pictured in the warm embrace of Tarvin. Here she is not the bold, brave, evil woman described above, but becomes an American Indian girl in love with a white man. Sitabhai keeps saying "White man loves money," "White man not afraid" like a fictional American Indian. In fact, Tarvin smiles at the unconscious Americanisms in her speech.[36]

This indicates that Wolcott Balestier, who collaborated with Kipling in *Naulahka*, not only wrote the first five chapters of the novel—chapters where the incidents take place in Topaz, Colorado—but also had a share in the writing of later chapters. Carrington suggests that Balestier might have written up the entire novel from the notes made by Kipling.[37] It can be safely assumed that he had a considerable share in the presentation of the gypsy queen, Sitabhai. In making her "Western," he has presented a distorted picture of the Indian woman.

The other Indian characters have neither sharpness of detail nor fullness of stature. The Maharaja Kunwara is an overdrawn, sentimental character. A mere pawn in the policies of the state, he is

[35] *Ibid.*, 285–286.
[36] *Ibid.*, 271.
[37] *The Life of Rudyard Kipling*, 140.

too passive, and his childish activities are more farce than sympathetic presentation of a prince's life. Dhunpat Rai, the Indian doctor, is cast in the mold typical of Kipling's Bengali characters. He is inefficient, lazy, and selfish. This is so stereotyped a picture that when Kipling mentions a native character we can safely predict that he will be a disreputable person.

Finally, the question remains: has the Christian hustled the Aryan brown? The answer is no. Kipling has not proved the thesis he set forth to prove. Tarvin's motives in coming to India are purely selfish. He wants the "Naulahka," because it can bring the railroad and thereby,

> He would be the saviour of his town; the boys at home would take the horses out of his carriage and drag him up Pennsylvania Avenue with their own hands; and town lots would sell next year in Topaz by the running inch.[38]

His second purpose is to be with Kate, the girl he wants to marry. Wealth and love lure him to India. He is ready to leave soon after realizing these desires. Tarvin behaves very crudely. He raves and rants at the Rhatore station, using a string of abusive adjectives. To stay in Rhatore, he lies, telling the unsuspecting Maharaja that he is going to find gold in the river Amet. Except for playing pachisi with the Maharaja, cursing and swearing at the Indians, making a trip to find out about the "Naulahka," and making love to the gypsy, he does nothing to "hustle the Aryan brown."

Kate is, of course, more idealistic. She wants to help the suffering Indian women. Her months of service in Rhatore are admirable, but with the first disappointment, when all the women leave the hospital, she gives up. She has been represented as a person with strong determination. Tarvin argues with her day and night trying to persuade her that her trip to India is not important. She is described as being under the powerful influence of religious and moral idealism. Yet when the hospital is deserted, she gives up her cause. She hears from the queen that she must be married, and only then can she help the world. With surprising passivity, she accepts this logic and leaves the state. It is impossible to believe this con-

[38] Kipling, *Naulahka*, 239.

tradictory feeling in a person—that one so devoted would give up so suddenly. It takes more than a few months to create understanding, faith, and love for cultural communication. Therefore, Kate, lacking maturity of outlook and thought, is revealed as a teen-age girl who, in an impulsive moment, had imagined herself as Florence Nightingale. Kate does not "hustle the Aryan brown" either.

The Estes family is the third group representative of the West. But they seem to spend their time finding excuses for their slow work rather than achieving concrete results. They make a very poor impression. They do not "hustle the Aryan brown."

Thus *Naulahka*, with no thesis attempted, a melodramatic plot, characters without realism, and lacking in aesthetic unity, is a poor and unimpressive work about India. It belongs in the category of trite, paper-back pulp novels about India, with multicolored covers, and the following inscription: "Strange, exotic adventure in India, quest for the fabulous jewel Naulahka, with all the mystery, barbarism and lust of a savage sub-continent."

Naulahka, at best, may have historical value. With the achievement of Indian independence in 1947 and the consequent change in political status from a subject dominion to a sovereign republic, the Indian native states underwent a thorough transformation. In the first place, the dichotomy that existed between the "native state" and "the Indian province" ceased to have any meaning. The smaller states merged with the larger states, and from a confused, varied and differing patchwork of 562 states, there emerge a more orderly and well-knit pattern of governable states. This consolidation linked the backward, out-of-the-way states to the more advanced ones, thereby infusing them with new life-blood. Autocratic rulers, irresponsible playboys and indifferent Maharajas no longer have a place of privilege. Constitutional government, social reforms, and increasing benefits from Western technology have become features of the new states. The princely state and the backward state of Kipling's day are of the past. Seen against this new and changing background, *Naulahka* assumes historic value, preserving, however crudely, a grim picture of a backward Indian state of the era.

VI

Kim and the Indian Synthesis

> *"All India is full of holy men stammering gospels in strange tongues; shaken and consumed in the fires of their own zeal; dreamers, babblers, and visionaries; as it has been from the beginning and will continue to the end."*
>
> —KIM.

THE NOVEL of Kipling's mature years, *Kim*, is his best work on India. T. S. Eliot shares this opinion and considers it to be Kipling's greatest work,[1] while Boris Ford holds the view that *Kim* is a mere boy's tale of adventure.[2] Both Lafcadio Hearn[3] and Cyril Falls[4] have described it as revealing the inner workings of the Secret Service in India during British rule. There is no doubt that *Kim* is a great book for boys, taking its place alongside Stevenson's *Treasure Island* and *Kidnapped*, and Mark Twain's *Adventures of Tom Sawyer*. *Kim* has the characteristic features of a boy's story: the lovable boy hero involved in a quest filled with adventure and intrigue. But unlike the usual boy's story, *Kim* has a spiritual aspect as well. From his participation with the Lama, though not in final acceptance, Kim emerges a sadder and better being. Also included is a picture of the "great game" of the secret service, which was

[1] "An Essay on Rudyard Kipling," *A Choice of Kipling's Verse*, 30.
[2] "A Case for Rudyard Kipling?" *The Importance of Scrutiny*, ed. by Eric Bentley, 331.
[3] *A History of English Literature*, II, 806.
[4] *Rudyard Kipling*, 162.

played continually to keep the foundations of the British Empire from disintegrating. But while the "great game" provides a background influencing the action, it never dominates the novel. Apart from all this, *Kim* is an attempt to interpret everyday life in India.

In comparison to *Kim*, Kipling's early Indian stories belong to a period of apprenticeship and preparation. In his short stories, Kipling concentrated on the abnormal and odd in Indian life, championed the cause of the British Tommy in *Barrack-Room Ballads*, and analyzed the inner workings of the Indian government in *Departmental Ditties*. But in *Kim* he attempts to take in the whole of India.

Many of his earlier themes are elaborated and incorporated into *Kim*. There is the brief, but vivid, picture of the Indian army; the tale of "Lispeth," from *Plain Tales From the Hills,* repeated in the story of the Lady of Shamlegh; the Anglo-Indian, the native and the official worlds providing backgrounds as they did in the short stories. Administering medicine in the guise of a charm to soothe and satisfy the Indian native, Jat, is an echo from the earlier story, "The Tomb of his Ancestors." Buddhism, whose scriptural tales— *The Jataka Tales*—supplied Kipling with a wealth of source material for his *Jungle Books* and *Just so Stories*, supplies the religious atmosphere in *Kim*. The theme had been hinted in a minor key in the story, "Namgay Doola," where an Irish soldier going native provides the main interest. Even Kim's yearning for the open road had been expressed previously in the character of Strickland, who, incidentally, makes a brief appearance in *Kim*. In "Miss Youghal's Sais" Police Officer Strickland is torn between the promise made his wife to stick with mere departmental routine and his desire to wander in the streets of India:

> Strickland was far too fond of his wife, just then, to break his word, but it was a sore trial to him; for the streets and the bazars, and the sounds in them, were full of meaning to Strickland, and these called to him to come back and take up his wanderings and discoveries. Some day, I will tell you how he broke his promise to help a friend.[5]

[5] Kipling, "Miss Youghal's Sais," *Plain Tales from the Hills*, 39.

Kim gathers together all the writer's past experiences and fuses them into a total picture of India, presented with judgment and maturity. Here Kipling is not the propagandist, but a sympathetic reporter, recalling his Indian days in fond memory.

Kim is the product of Kipling's middle age, the period when he was in the process of settling down, a turning point in his life. In 1898, Sir Edward Burne Jones, Kipling's dear "Uncle Ned," died suddenly. Before the year was over, Kipling's sister Trix lost her mind. The following year Kipling fell seriously ill, an event which caused great concern the world over. The same year his beloved daughter Josephine died. Increasing this domestic gloom, war broke out in South Africa. Kipling saw in the South African Boer War a threat to the type of empire-builder that he had idealized, men who were guided by new and challenging ideals:

> He shall come back on his own track, and
>   by his scarce-cooled camp.
> There shall he meet the roaring street,
>   the derrick and the stamp:
> There he shall blaze a nation's ways with
>   hatchet and with brand,
> Till on his lost-won wilderness an Empire's
>   outposts stand![6]

Kipling's personal friend, Cecil Rhodes, who shared with him dreams of the empire, was in the town of Kimberley when the Boers attacked it. Therefore the Boer War touched at several points that were close and intimate to Kipling. His views, his ideals, and his vision were at stake.

The personal loss that Kipling had suffered in the domestic tragedies mentioned above was increased by what was happening in South Africa. He plunged furiously into the Boer War controversy, becoming a pamphleteer and an uncompromising propagandist, denouncing in the most bitter terms Kruger and all that he stood for. His political writings of this period, from "The Absent Minded Beggar" to "The Islanders," are one continuous barrage of

[6] "The Voortrekker," *Rudyard Kipling's Verse*, 556.

propaganda expounding the supremacy of the British Empire and sounding the call for Englishmen to take up the burden.

With the end of the war, Kipling's mood changed. After the bitterness, heat, and loss of life, Kipling felt an imperative need to settle down to a life of serenity and calm. Like Kim, he felt weary following his domestic and national calamities. With his realization of loss, Kipling was able to express amiable sentiments after the Boer War. In "The Settler," bitterness and prejudice are forgotten; a spirit of tolerance, forgiveness and co-operation is reflected:

> Here in a large and sunlit land,
>   Where no wrong bites to the bone,
> I will lay my hand in my neighbour's hand,
>   And together we will atone
> For the set folly and the red breach
>   And the black waste of it all;
> Giving and taking counsel each
>   Over the cattle-kraal.[7]

It was during this period and in this mood that *Kim* was written and published. Kipling may have asked himself the question that Kim was to ask of himself in the novel, "Who is Kim—Kim—Kim?" In growing old, in evaluating the past, Kipling turned back to the best years of his life, the Indian years, when everything was secure and the family square intact. *Kim* is his last word on India, in which he relives those Indian years. The yearning of Kim for the open road, for its smells, sights, and sounds is part of the longing of Kipling himself. He was intimately familiar with many of the roads along which Kim accompanied the Lama. In *Something of Myself* Kipling wrote:

Between us, (his father) we knew every step, sight and smell on his casual road, as well as the persons he met. Once only I remember, did I have to bother the India office, where there are four acres of books and documents in the basements, for a certain work on Indian magic which I always sincerely regret that I could not steal.[8]

[7] "The Settler," *ibid.*, 212.
[8] *Something of Myself*, 135.

The strong nostalgic quality of *Kim* reveals Kipling's own love for India.

That Kipling had made an earlier attempt to write a novel about India is revealed in a letter he wrote from Simla to Miss Edith Macdonald:

> Further I have really embarked to the tune of 237 foolscap pages on my novel—Mother Maturin—an Anglo-Indian episode. Like Topsy "it growed" while I wrote and I find myself now committed to a two volume business at least. It's not one bit nice or proper but it carries a grim sort of a moral with it and tries to deal with the unutterable horrors of lower class Eurasian and native life as they exist outside reports and reports and reports. I haven't got the Pater's verdict on what I've done. He comes up in a couple of days and will then sit in judgment. Trixie says it's awfully horrid; Mother says it's nasty but powerful and I know it to be in large measure true. It is an unfailing delight to me and I'm just in that pleasant stage where the characters are living with me always. The parents say "publish it at home and let it have a chance." I hold that India would be the better place and have already received one offer for the book from an Indian Paper.[9]

This indicates that in 1885 Kipling was still interested in the grotesque, the horrible, and the abnormal in Indian life, themes he had used extensively in his short stories. Kipling worked on *Mother Maturin* for years, accumulating material, but "it remained in solution in his notebooks, an unwritten masterpiece." Mrs. Hill, a very close friend of Kipling, had read the novel and gives the following account of it, the only account available dealing with the thematic contents:

> *Mother Maturin* I have read, which was never published because John Lockwood Kipling was not satisfied with it. It is the story of an old Irishwoman who kept an opium den in Lahore but sent her daughter to be educated in England. She married a Civilian and came to live in Lahore—hence a story how Government secrets came to be known in the Bazaar and vice versa.[10]

[9] Carrington, *The Life of Rudyard Kipling*, 52–53.
[10] American Art Association, *Catalogue of English and American Authors* (New York, 1921), 42.

The idea of opium addicts held a fascination for Kipling. His very first short story, "A Gate of a Thousand Sorrows," takes place in an opium den, and Kim's father dies an opium addict.

Judging from the theme and the unutterable horror which was to have characterized *Mother Maturin*, it was well that Kipling waited until he was mature enough to write a novel like *Kim*.

There is something special and different about the way *Kim* was written. Most of Kipling's writings were the result of his journalistic ventures. Even some of his finest stories, "The Man Who Would Be King" and "The Finest Story in the World," are basically skillful reporting. All the techniques for making a tale stand up are clearly evident. There is an efficiency about them directed toward making the stories slick and effective. Consequently there emerges a stereotyped picture of India—of heat and dust, cunning, cowardly Bengalis, faithful but revengeful servants. There is no growth of sensibilities in the stories. Boris Ford criticizes the novel, *Kim*, as also deficient in expression of sensibility or emotional development. We cannot agree with Ford, for these qualities are present in three respects: in the conception itself, in Kipling's own personality and feeling for India, and in the conception and development of the two main characters, Kim and the venerable Teshoo Lama.

Kim was in Kipling's mind as early as 1897. In *Something of Myself* he tells us:

> Now even in the Bliss Cottage I had a vague notion of an Irish boy, born in India and mixed up with native life. I went as far as to make him the son of a private in an Irish battalion, and christened him "Kim of the Rishti"—short, that is, for Irish. This done, I felt like Mr. Micawber that I had as good as paid that I.O.U. on the future and went after other things for some years.[11]

But *Kim* returned with insistence and as the novel came to be written, the character of Kim threatened to get out of hand and had to be kept within bounds. Never before had a character dominated Kipling, he had always controlled them with confident practicality. Hence, when he admits the great siege on his heart and mind by

[11] *Something of Myself*, 133.

Kim, it is indicative of emotional growth. Written under the influence of his daemon, the novel is a work of inspired imagination.[12]

In examining the two main characters, Kim and the Lama, we find a definite growth and increasing awareness. They pass through a process of self-education. Kim, whose superiority of race is emphasized throughout the novel, states at the end, after his association with the Lama:

> Thou hast said there is neither black nor white, why plague me with this talk, Holy One? Let me rub the other foot. It vexes me, I am *not* a Sahib. I am thy Chela, and my head is heavy on my shoulders.[13]

This is an unusual admission for Kim, who had prided himself on being a sahib. In the past he had critically questioned the philosophy of passivity, saying that action was his guiding principle. We find him at the beginning of the novel sitting on the great gun, Zam-Zammeh. Only he can sit on this gun, because he is English and the English are masters of the Punjab. The other Hindu and Moslem boys who play with Kim are subservient to him. He is the boss of the street boys. But gradually Kim grows to realize that there is much he can and must learn from others. A turning point seems to come when Lurgan Sahib has Kim and the Hindu boy match wits in an observation and memory game. Kim acknowledges his deficiencies, and learns for ten days from the Hindu boy, to whom he said earlier, "I hate you, I hate all Hindus." Kim's progress in life depends upon the co-operation of several people. It is the Lama's money that gets him an English education. From the Bengali, Babu Hurree Chunder Mookerjee, he learns of the "great game." His own men, Lurgan Sahib and Colonel Creighton, contribute their share to his development. Then there is Mahbub Ali, his mentor and friend, who first instills in him a love for the secret and for intrigue. Kim's recognition of the contribution to his education made by several people is part of the growth of his character.

Even the Lama undergoes a change of character. He is involved in a quest for the River of Arrow. This great purpose, to which

12 *Ibid.*, 201.
13 Kipling, *Kim*, 443.

he has dedicated himself, is all-absorbing. The search for the physical appearance of the River clouds his spiritual vision. He finally realizes that the River is not somewhere else, but at his very feet, if he has the faith to see it. He says:

> So thus the search is ended. For the merit that I have acquired, the River of the Arrow is here. It broke forth at our feet, as I have said. I have found it.[14]

Thus Kipling reveals maturity in his delineation of these two principal characters. They do not become mere types, the Indian boy and the Oriental holy man, but rather retain a distinctive individuality, moving toward an awareness of themselves and their surroundings, an awareness such as Kipling himself had finally achieved.

After reading *Kim*, one may ask how much of the novel actually is Indian. The locale is India, the crowded figures are Indian, but the important points of the novel outline a different situation. Kim is of Irish parentage, a fact made clear at the very beginning of the novel:

> Though he was burned black as any native; though he spoke the vernacular by preference, and his mother tongue in a clipped uncertain sing-song; though he consorted on terms of perfect equality with the small boys of the bazaar; Kim was white—a poor white of the very poorest.[15]

The venerable Teshoo Lama is Tibetan, not Indian. The main religious fervor of the novel is Buddhism, not Hinduism, the major religious force of India. Most of the story takes place in a limited locale in India, the northwestern provinces. Therefore, it seems as though there is not much of India in the novel.

But *Kim*, for all these seeming diversities, is Indian to the core. In the character of Kim, despite his Irish ancestry, Kipling has created a perfect specimen of the Indian boy. The daily habits, customs and attitudes of a poor, Indian, low-caste street boy are recorded with skill and understanding. Yet he possesses some Irish

[14] *Ibid.*, 473.
[15] *Ibid.*, 3.

characteristics, like his sense of humor and curiosity. We read that he had a deadly fear of snakes, for "no native training can quench the white man's horror of the serpent." Later in the story, when the Russian strikes the Lama, the blow awakens "every unknown Irish devil" in Kim, and he attacks the Russian with fury. Except for these few and scattered Irish, or white man's, traits, he is as true a representative of an Indian street boy as can be found.

Brought up by the half-caste Indian woman, Kim finds the open Indian street, with all its color and excitement, his natural habitation. Here he mixes freely with the natives, becomes one of them, acquires their characteristics, and feels completely at home in native Indian life. Like other Indian boys, he is suspicious of missionaries and "white men of serious aspect." They are incapable of seeing the beauty of the city of Lahore, which Kim loves as only a native can. Later, when he is found by Reverend Mr. Bennett and sent to school, he expresses the desire to be free and among his people. When Mahbub Ali asks him the question, "And who are thy people?" he replies unhesitatingly, "This great and beautiful land." Kim is "The Little Friend of All the World," on intimate acquaintance with all kinds of people—policemen, beggars, and holy men.

He participates in the crowded activities of the Indian street for the sheer excitement of it. We find him performing secret missions for sleek young men of fashion, crying lustily at the heels of marriage processions, and well versed in the several techniques of begging. In fact, he is a "master beggar" who studies his customers and suits his approach to their mood. He plays upon their emotions. To those with sentimental hearts, he emphasizes his unfortunate status as an orphan. Some believe in supernatural forces; for their benefit Kim poses as an astrologer and palmist, foretelling their future, the proportions of bad and good depending on the size of their charity. In some, fear brings out the quality of mercy, so he threatens these people with curses; while to those who believe in religion, he uses "religion" as a charm to woo them into giving him alms. In several cases he demands charity as a commission, almost his birth-right, "that immemorial commission of Asia," for services rendered, like protecting a shop from a bull. And like most of the

Indian street boys, he always begs in the name of a holy man. By befriending the Lama, Kim gains in power, for the Lama is an unusually splendid example of a holy man. Kim displays his new-found treasure to best advantage.

Borrowing freely from the customs of every part of the country, Kim typifies the true spirit of the Indian street boy, to whom the whole country is one, and all Indian roads the promise and fulfillment of a search for adventure and excitement. *Kim* was written in 1901, but even today one can find counterparts of Kim in any Indian city. This is the first and almost the very last intimate picture of an Indian street boy.

We meet with another problem with respect to the use of Buddhism in *Kim*. The question immediately arises, why didn't Kippling select a Hindu priest or a Muslim Moulvi, why should it have been the Buddhist monk? Since Hinduism and Islam are the two major religions of India, the question is appropriate.

We have already discovered, in Kipling's short stories, the fascination he felt toward the Muslims of the North. Their rugged outdoor life and their emphasis on action attracted Kipling. Having lived the greater part of his Indian life in the North, he had come to understand the Muslims much better than he did the Hindus. As a result, he reveals the Muslim in a more favorable light than the Hindu. But in *Kim*, written during his struggle for synthesis, there was no room for personal likes and prejudices. A middle ground was necessary, and in Buddhism, with its castelessness, purity, and austerity, he found the golden mean. This appeal for moderation and tolerance, such as Kipling himself had learned over the years, is the dominant theme of *Kim*. It sets the tone of the entire novel:

> Oh ye who tread the Narrow Way,
> By Tophet-flare to Judgment Day,
> Be gentle when the heathen pray
> To Buddha at Kamakura![16]

In spite of the fact that Buddhism spread from India to other lands,

[16] *Ibid.*

India is its spiritual home. It enjoyed recognition and patronage in India during the fourteenth century, and alone among all other religions came close to being a state religion under the Indian ruler Asoka. Buddhism's stern belief in the philosophy of non-violence left an abiding impression on the Indian character. Thus in selecting it to be the main religious fervor of the novel, Kipling is not skirting the fringe of Indian life.

The religious spirit of India is equally well represented in the personality of the Lama. The Lama is Tibetan, and Tibetans, we are told by Fosco Mariani in his book *Secret Tibet*, are the least oriental of all orientals. Big, noisy, and expansive they are, "men made to stride like giants over their endless plateaux, always ready to drink, sing, or believe in a miracle; merchants, bandits, monks and shepherds."[17] But the venerable Teshoo Lama in *Kim* is a symbol of spiritual force, and this makes him part of India because, as Mariani perceptively points out, "the origin of practically every spiritual motif in Tibetan civilisation is to be sought in India."[18] Hence the Lama, in returning to India is revisiting his spiritual homeland, the cradle and source of his faith. Thus, in a technical but unimportant sense, he is "Tibetan," although in the larger and more meaningful sense of representing the religious spirit of India, which he is expected to do, he is universal. Follower of the middle way, he has no caste, no color, no sect. Within the broad ethical framework of pursuing the path of righteousness, Tibetan monks had their own individual moral codes. According to a Tibetan proverb, "Every village its own dialect. Every Lama his own doctrine."[19] Thus there is flexibility in the personality of Teshoo Lama, and it helped Kipling to present his own ideal conception of the holy man.

It is in the personality of the Lama that the theme of *Kim* is expressed. The imperishable quality of the novel lies in exploration of the topic of religion and its abiding influence on the people of India. To the extent that this theme is developed in the nature of the Lama,

---

[17] *Secret Tibet*, 43.
[18] *Ibid.*, 65.
[19] *Ibid.*, 85.

he becomes the pivotal character in the novel. It is only with the appearance of the Lama that the action in *Kim* starts to take shape.

The novel opens with a typically realistic picture of an Indian city street, with its quiet round of daily activities carried on in a mood of leisureliness. We see Kim, perched on top of the great gun Zam-Zammeh, in front of the museum or "Wonder House," playing with all his Muslim and Hindu friends, rich and poor alike, "for India is the only democratic country in the world."[20] But the picture quickens and awakes to greater life with the appearance of the venerable Teshoo Lama. His strangeness, both in appearance and in outlook, captivates the playful boys, and Kim decides to investigate him "precisely as he would have investigated a new building or a strange festival in Lahore City."[21] The Lama not only captures Kim's attention, taking him away from his play, but thereafter dominates the entire novel, guiding it with force and dignity. It is through him that Kipling effects the course and direction of the novel.

The prospective development of the novel is revealed in the opening chapter of *Kim*, in connection with the conversation between the Lama and the Englishman who is the curator of the museum. The Lama is no mere layman, but a great Buddhist scholar who has held the honored post of abbot of Suchzen monastery in Tibet. But his deep and cloistered study of Buddhism has made him neither a pedant nor a fundamentalist searching for religion only in the words of the Scriptures, thereby following the letter and not the spirit. In fact, learning and living at the monastery have contributed only to an awareness of himself and his surroundings. All this book knowledge, resulting only in conflicting interpretations by different priests because of their own egotism, he has come to recognize as being merely illusion and vanity—"Maya," as he calls it. He expresses his dissatisfaction to the curator of the museum:

> The books of my Lamassery I read, and they were as dried pith; and the later ritual with which we of the Reformed Law have cum-

[20] Kipling, *Kim*, 8.
[21] *Ibid.*, 22.

bered ourselves—that, too, had no worth to these old eyes. Even the followers of the Excellent One are at feud on feud with one another. It is an illusion.[22]

Attempting to discover the reality behind this illusion, he has come to his spiritual homeland, India, where he will strive anew to achieve his goal.

His devout purpose, as is that of all Buddhists, is to free himself "from the wheel of things."[23] This he attempts "by a most broad and open road,"[24] which, in this case, is retracing the wanderings of Buddha, in order to find the River of Arrow, for "whoso bathes in it washes away all taint and speckle of sin."[25] But the River of Arrow is only symbolic, it represents the Lama's inner desire to go to the very life-springs of Buddhism and its meaning. The Englishman shows him a map, indicating the wanderings of Buddha:

> Then he was shown a mighty map, spotted and traced with yellow. The brown finger followed the curator's pencil from point to point. Here was Kapilavastu, here the Middle kingdom, and here Mahabodhi, the Mecca of Buddhism; and here was Kusinagara, sad place of the Holy One's death.[26]

With the aid of this map, the Lama is going to retrace the very movements of the Excellent One. This is going to be the course of the novel, with the Lama leading his readers on the search. All other incidents and episodes in the novel are going to be subservient to this main theme, a religious search.

The Lama's journey with Kim helps the secret service, for when Mahbub Ali entrusts to Kim a piece of paper bearing some valuable information he knows that:

> A wandering Lama with a low-caste boy-servant might attract a moment's interest as they wandered about India, the land of pilgrims; but no one would suspect, or what was more to the point, rob them.[27]

22 *Ibid.*, 16.
23 *Ibid.*, 17.
24 *Ibid.*
25 *Ibid.*
26 *Ibid.*, 15.
27 *Ibid.*, 39.

The plot of the "great game," wherein the Indian government is engaged in hunting down rebels against the British rule in India, hinges on the Lama's pilgrimage for its existence. In fact, this plot is barely mentioned in the opening chapter, and, as Carrington aptly points out, Kipling does not take the trouble to elaborate on it. The next time we read of this "great game," we find that it has ended. It is the journey of the Lama that is important. The other episodes, such as Kim's educational experiences in St. Xavier's, and the Russian machinations in the northwest of India, happen as results of the journey. Even the Indian panorama, with its vastness and variety, which *Kim* so impressively portrays, unfolds as we follow the Lama in his many wanderings.

The theme "search" is emphasized in the novel, with the Lama's search for the River of Arrow being dominant. There is also Kim's search for the "Red Bull on the Green Plain," that of the secret service for the five kings and their plot, and the vast, diverse group of Indian pilgrims on their quest for peace of mind along the Grand Trunk Road. Behind all this was the mind and spirit of Kipling himself seeking peace. Attempting to secure this, he traveled in imagination to the scene of his happiest days—his boyhood days in India.

In this theme of quest for peace of mind, the theme of the pilgrimage constituting the religious motif, Kipling has not only placed his fingers on the pulse of India, but has captured its very heartbeat. Religion plays a dominant part in Indian life. India has been the cradle of some of the great religions of the world, and she has been a foster mother for practically all the faiths.

The Lama's main activity is his pilgrimage in search of the River of Arrow. Now Hindus are much given to pilgrimage. Holy places, where saints, mystics, and philosophers received their inspirations and revelations of "divine truth" are found all over the country. Both duty and sheer pleasure of travel inspire millions of Indians to visit these holy places each year. The great life line of India, the Grand Trunk Road described in *Kim*, is, even today, crowded for most of the year with men, women, and children journeying to holy places. Indian religious history records not only how the common people received inspiration at these places, but also that even saints found greater strength by visiting and meditating at the traditionally honored sacred places. Swami Pavitrananda, in the article "Pilgrimage and Fairs: Their bearing on Indian life," in *The Cultural Heritage of India*, mentions the impact of sacred places on Indian saints:

> Sankara had some of his realizations at Benares. Chaitanya Deva found the image of Jagannatha at Puri so very living that he was about to embrace the deity. Ramadas saw the vision of Ramachandra at the temple of Pandharpur. Tulsidas had his realizations at Chitrakut. Sri Ramakrishna saw many wonderful visions at Dakshineshwara, Benares, Brindaban and other holy places.[28]

All these names produce a magical effect upon the Indian mind, and a visit to these places becomes a passion and a necessity with them. Furthermore Kipling has shown keen insight into Indian life by making the pilgrimage of the Lama the dominant one. Swami Pavitrananda points out that the Hindus acquired the practice of conducting pilgrimages by observing the Buddhist monks in India.[29] Thus it is only natural that the Lama take the spotlight in this journey. Kipling captures the spirit of the nation when he writes in *Kim:*

> All India is full of holy men stammering gospels in strange tongues; shaken and consumed by the fires of their own zeal; dreamers, babblers, and visionaries; as it has been from the beginning and will continue to the end.[30]

Because of this great respect shown toward men of holy aspect and Christ-like personality, India was able to produce a man like Gandhi, who preached non-violence to the nation, and a man like Bhave, appropriately called by Hallam Tennyson "The Walking Saint of India,"[31] who walks across the Indian sub-continent preaching his strange but highly successful gospel, "I have come

[28] "Pilgrimage and Fairs: Their Bearing on Indian Life," *The Cultural Heritage of India*, III (Calcutta, 1936), 157.

[29] *Ibid.*, 156.

[30] *Kim*, 54.

[31] *India's Walking Saint: The Story of Vinobha Bhave*, 70.

to loot you with love."[32] Thus *Kim,* written in 1901, still has a direct relationship to contemporary India as it touches upon that dominant quality of Indian life, religion and respect for men of holy behavior. This concern gives *Kim* its imperishable quality.

Pilgrimages have brought about catholicity of outlook, while religion itself has diffused noble qualities of charity and friendship among the Indian people. In the short story, "Georgie Porgie," Kipling described India as the most charitable country in the world,[33] and in *Kim* he stresses the effect of religion on the people, making them a kindly and charitable group. "It is a kindly land."[34] "This is a good land—the land of the South," says the Lama, and it is he, representing the religious force, who serves to draw forth these qualities from the Indian people.

The Lama, belonging to another faith and coming from another country, is, to a certain extent, an "outsider" in India. Yet people forget his alien quality, since he represents the true religious holy mind and spirit. Wherever he goes, he receives hospitality and reverent treatment, for they see in the Lama a man passionately devoted to the search for God. Kim has no difficulty in obtaining food, for the Lama's presence makes people charitable. In the crowded Indian train, carrying pilgrims of all creeds and sects to different parts of the country, the Lama becomes the center of attraction. They make way for him and listen tolerantly to his story of the Buddha. Whenever there is an opportunity, the Lama makes use of that chance to pray and gently preach the doctrine of the "Middle Way." People invite him to their homes, feeling deeply honored when he accepts their invitation. Even Mahbub Ali, the hardy Pathan, pays tribute to the righteousness of the Lama.[35] Kipling had, in the story "Miracle of Puran Bhagat," already revealed the devotion that the Indian people show to holy men. The truly religious spirit of brotherhood and charity binds the people together and generates a spirit of tolerance, which shows the fundamental unity of India despite its apparent diversity. In

[32] *Ibid.,* 65.
[33] "Georgie Porgie," *Life's Handicap,* 70.
[34] *Kim,* 58.
[35] *Ibid.,* 468.

recognizing and presenting this aspect, Kipling shows an understanding of India in *Kim*.

Bound up with the theme of religion and forming an integral part of Indian spiritual life is the disciple and teacher relationship, which Kipling presents with insight and understanding in the novel. The life of no holy man, Hindu or Buddhist, is complete without a chela or disciple, with the pupil respecting his preceptor as a father, living with him, accompanying him on his pilgrimages, and serving him with devotion and sincerity. In fact, holy men considered a chela a necessity, looking upon a good chela as a gift from heaven, sent to assist them in their task.

The Lama frequently expresses this belief in speaking of his relationship with Kim. "He is my disciple," he tells Mahbub Ali. "He was sent, I think, to guide me to that river. Sitting under a gun was I when he came suddenly. Such things have befallen the fortunate to whom guidance was allowed."[36] He goes a step farther and sees in their relationship a link from pre-existence. Kim and he could have been friends in a previous life, and to support his view he narrates a tale from the *Jatakas*. This is the tale of the friendship between an elephant and a dog, who had been friends in a previous existence as human beings.[37] Kim, helping the Lama, is possibly the reward for a good deed that the Lama performed in his previous life. With deep sincerity and abundant faith born out of righteous living, he tells Kim:

> Perhaps in a former life it was permitted that I should have rendered thee some service. May be (he smiled) I freed thee from a trap; or, having caught thee on a hook in the days when I was not enlightened, cast thee back into the river again.[38]

It is no superficial relationship, such as one might find between any orphan beggar boy and a holy man, but is deeply significant, with a spiritual aspect. In presenting the disciple and teacher relationship in this light, Kipling has focused attention on a dominant feature of Indian religious life and also on an important aspect of traditional

[36] *Ibid.*, 34.
[37] *Ibid.*, 316.
[38] *Ibid.*, 116.

Indian education. The traditional Hindu educational pattern, still existing in some of the sacred places of India, glorified and emphasized the harmonious relationship between the teacher and the taught. In some cases, an entire "school" or "university" consisted of just one teacher and one student. This was the famed "Guru-Kula-Ashrama" type of learning by living with the teacher and his family. The spirit of this system is carried out, in part, by the Lama and Kim.

Kim joins the Lama out of curiosity and in order to satisfy his thirst for a life of excitement. But gradually he feels the impact of the peaceful and serene personality of the Lama, and under its influence surrenders himself to his master. He becomes an ideal disciple and, as the old woman in *Kim* states, "Beggars a plenty have I met, and holy men to boot, but never such a *yogi* nor such a disciple."[39] Boris Ford in his essay "A Case for Kipling?" states that Kipling has created the Lama only to help Kim in his role in the "great game." He accuses Kim of selfishness.[40] This charge is not valid and seems to indicate that Boris Ford has not familiarized himself intimately with the novel. The relationship between the two is ideal, and after Kim wanders with the Lama, the "great game" becomes merely incidental. While Colonel Creighton and Mahbub Ali teach Kim some of the technicalities involved in the "great game," his spiritual and moral awakening is the direct result of the Lama's influence. From the playful boy that he is at the beginning, he develops into a mature individual by the end of the novel. When the Lama asks if he wishes to leave him, Kim sternly replies, "No, I am not a dog or a snake to bite when I have learned to love."[41]

It is true that finally he chooses a life of action, by joining the secret service, in preference to the life of contemplation that the Lama represents. But the Lama himself approves this life, and Kim enters the "great game" not merely as one who knows the rules, but as an individual with a deeper understanding of the experience

[39] *Ibid.*, 58.
[40] "A Case for Rudyard Kipling?" *The Importance of Scrutiny*, 327.
[41] Kipling, *Kim*, 444.

and meaning of life. He faces a conflict before he makes up his mind to select his career. The conflict itself is a result of his maturity, gained by his association with and appreciation of the Lama. To him, the "great game" becomes not merely a proper career for white sahibs, but one of responsibility, requiring human understanding. Furthermore, who is a "Sahib"? Kipling here takes a very broad and tolerant view. The Lama says that he may have been a sahib in his previous life, and the curator of the museum may have been the honored Abbot of Such-Zen monastery. After all, this external form, native or "Sahib," is only one of the many "tricks of the stupid carcass— shadow changing to another shadow."[42] There remains no black or white, but mutual help and affection. "Thou leanest on me in the body, Holy One, but I lean on thee for all other things," says Kim to the Lama. The Lama says, when Mahbub Ali, tells him of Kim's desire to join the "great game":

> To that end he was prepared. I acquired merit in that I gave alms for his sake. A good deed does not die. He aided me in my Search. I aided him in his. Just the Wheel, O horse-seller from the North. Let him be a teacher. Let him be a scribe. What matter? He will have attained Freedom at the end. The rest is illusion.[43]

Therefore, Kim, has his master's complete approval in his new career.

While *Kim* discloses the Indian religious spirit in general, it touches more specifically on Buddhism, which finds its interpreter in the Lama. Kipling was, as we have noted earlier, in a mood to see India not in terms of mere black and white, but in terms of synthesis and harmony. Buddhism, with its middle way, its Indian origin but international acceptance, appealed to him. Buddhism is India's distinctive contribution to Asia, as Fosco Maraini writes in *Secret Tibet:*

> India is the Greece of Asia. India was for the East what Greece was for the West, for us; that is to say, the birth place of all the philosophic ideas and all the influences in art and poetry which for

[42] *Ibid.,* 443.
[43] *Ibid.,* 446.

thousands of years determined, and to an extent still determine, the intellectual life of millions of men. Moreover, India was something else as well. Greece did not give to Western civilization the religion that subsequently became its very life blood, but in Buddhism India gave to the Asiatic Continent its most tremendous civilizing influence.[44]

Kipling was attempting to demonstrate the universality of Indian civilization, and he rightfully selected the gentle, venerable Teshoo Lama, a man untouched by caste and prejudice, to represent it. That *Kim* is redolent with the spirit of Buddhism, its myth and legend, symbols and philosophy, constitutes another of its imperishable qualities.

The Lama represents Tibetan Buddhism or Lamaism. Lamaism is an important religious complex within the wider orbit of Buddhism. From one point of view, because of its rites and institutions culminating in a pope, the Dalai Lama, it could be said to correspond to Roman Catholicsim in the Christian world. However, Lamaism is recent, dating from the seventh and subsequent centuries of our era. It will not be wrong to say, considering the vast amount of myth and symbolism associated with Lamaism, that Tibetan Buddhism represents the romantic and aesthetic aspects of ascetic Buddhism as it flourished in India. It appealed to Kipling's romantic and aesthetic sensibilities, for his hero—the Lama—besides being a Buddhist, "was an artist, as well as a wealthy abbot in his own place."[45]

Kipling evokes the exotic world of Lamaism by reference to some of its more outstanding symbols. The most noted is the Tibetan "Wheel of Life," rich in color and philosophic symbolism. Tracing the "Wheel of Life" in all its subtle and meaningful lines is an art known to a select few in Tibet, and the venerable Teshoo Lama has mastered it. In describing it, Kipling recalls a bygone opulent era of Lamaism:

> He drew from under the table a sheet of strangely scented yellow Chinese paper, the brushes, and the slab of India ink. In cleanest,

[44] *Secret Tibet*, 26.
[45] *Kim*, 395.

severest outline he had traced the Great Wheel with its six spokes, whose centre is the conjoined Hog, Snake, and Dove (Ignorance, Anger, and Lust), and whose compartments are all the heavens and hells, and all the chances of human life. Men say that the Bodhisat Himself first drew it with grains of rice upon dust, to teach His disciples the cause of things. Many ages have crystallised it into a most wonderful convention crowded with hundreds of little figures whose every line carries a meaning. Few can translate the picture parable; there are not twenty in all the world who can draw it surely without a copy; of those who can both draw and expound are but three.[46]

The "Wheel of Life" is like a compass guiding the boat of the Lama's life. Its symbolic chart and allegorical quality presents the Lamaist code of ethics, after which he patterns his own life. "The boat of his Soul staggers," when he swerves from its path. Thus when the Lama confronts the Russian who tears up the "Wheel of Life," the effect on the Lama's spiritual personality is very disturbing. He interprets this brutal act by the Russian as a result of his own sinning. It is among the hills that he encounters this incident, while searching for the River of Arrow. The Lama knows that his wanderings in the hills are not a part of his real search, for "the Arrow fell in the plains—not in the hills. Therefore, what do we here?" questions the Lama.[47] He has come to the hills out of personal, "selfish" desire, thereby committing the deadliest of Buddhist sins, that of succumbing to the desires of the flesh. He has swerved from the "Wheel of Life":

> My stupid body yearned to the hills and the snow of the hills, down below there . . . . They strengthened me to do evil, to forget my Search. I delighted in life and the lust of life. I desired strong slopes to climb. I cast about to find them. I measured the strength of my body, which is evil, against the high hills. I made a mock of thee (Kim) when thy breath came short under Jamnotri. I jested when thou wouldst not face the snow of the pass.[48]

[46] *Ibid.*, 314–15.
[47] *Ibid.*, 428.
[48] *Ibid.*, 426.

The Lama reveals ignorance and lust, both forbidden by the "Wheel of Life," and, as he explains,

> Ignorance and Lust met Ignorance and Lust upon the road, and they begat Anger. The blow was a sign to me, who am no better than a strayed *Yak*, that my place is not here.[49]

Therefore, he wishes to turn back to the plains and to his search.

There is an interrelationship between the "Wheel of Life" and the destiny of the Lama. The rent that the Russian made on the chart is a physical reflection of the inward severance of the Lama's own life. The "Wheel of Life" is torn to its very end, and hangs by its last joined piece. The life of the Lama, like the "Wheel of Life" has almost reached its end. He shows the chart to Kim, explaining its fantastic symbolic significance:

> There remains untorn by the idolater no more than the breadth of my finger-nail. So much, then, is the span of my life in this body. I have served the Wheel all my days. Now the Wheel serves me. . . . Is it plain, *Chela?* Kim started at the brutally disfigured chart. From left to right diagonally the rent ran—from the Eleventh House where desire gives birth to the child (as it is drawn by Buddhists)—across the human and animal worlds, to the Fifth House—the empty house of the senses. The logic was unanswerable.[50]

Kipling reveals in this incident of the "Wheel of Life" something of the rich world of symbolism and metaphysical phantasmagoria that are part of Lamaism.

Kipling also portrays in the Lama another trait of Lamaism, the longing for the aesthetic together with the ascetic. The reader's first glimpse of the venerable Teshoo Lama reveals an artist who feels a rapturous delight at seeing the Greco-Buddhist sculpture in the Wonder House. He enters the museum and experiences a sense of reverent elation at the life of Buddha interpreted in stone and frescoes:

> Here was the devout Asita, the pedant of Simeon in the Christian story, holding the Holy Child on his knee while mother and father listened; and here were incidents in the legend of the cousin Deva-

[49] *Ibid.,* 427.   [50] *Ibid.,* 428.

datta; here was the wicked woman who accused the Master of impurity, all confounded; here was the teaching in the Deer-park; the miracle that stunned the fire-worshippers; here was the Bodhisat in royal state as a prince; the miraculous birth; the death at Kushinagara, where the weak disciple fainted; while there were almost countless repetitions of the meditation under the Bodhi tree; and the adoration of the alms bowl was everywhere. "'Tis all here. A treasure locked," said the Lama.[51]

In the above passage Kipling highlights some of the most significant events in the life of the Buddha, which is once again in keeping with the religious atmosphere of *Kim*, and he also indicates the fascination art holds for the Lama. Lamaism classifies the life of Buddha into twelve major episodes, and Fosco Maraini points out their influence on Tibetan life:

> The Twelve Episodes of the Life (of the Buddha) provide one of the themes which have most frequently inspired Tibetan artists. They deal with this theme in twelve scenes, often divided into two big frescoes or grouped into one big one.[52]

In spite of the austerity of Lamaism, the aesthetic is an integral part of the faith. The Lama finds symbolic meaning in his very first meeting with these Buddhist sculptures: "My pilgrimage is well begun. And what work! What work!"[53]

With all this, as with the brief but vivid reference to "Tibetan devil-dance masks, hanging above the fiend-embroidered draperies of those ghastly functions—horned masks, scowling masks, and masks of idiotic terror"[54] found in Mr. Lurgan's house, Kipling re-creates in Kim a truly Tibetan atmosphere. Tibet is as important as India in the novel, for it is equally religious. "In Tibet, everything begins and ends with Religion," writes Tsung-Lien Shen in *Tibet and the Tibetans*, which re-emphasizes the religious motif of *Kim*.[55]

[51] *Ibid.*, 14–15.
[52] *Secret Tibet*, 68.
[53] Kipling, *Kim*, 12.
[54] *Ibid.*, 244.
[55] Tsung-Lien-Shen and Shen-Chi-Liu, *Tibet and Tibetans* (California, 1953), 66.

The philosophic aspect of Buddhism is also present in the personality of the Lama. Kipling does not discuss any of its metaphysical problems, but he clearly states some of its fundamental concepts.

The Buddhist faith is divided into two sects, the Hinayana and the Mahayana. The Lama, being a Tibetan, belongs to the Mahayana group, to whom two ways are open to gain Nirvana. One is Sutra, the exoteric course, which is shared by the Hinayana sect, and the other Tantra, the esoteric course. Both are found in the sacred Buddhist scriptures, the Tripitakas. The esoteric course is mainly concerned with matters of ritual, mystical and magic ways of acquiring occult powers, the use and meaning of formulas and enchantments, the use of letters of the alphabet, esoteric diagrams and talismans, and the symbolism of gestures.[56]

The venerable Teshoo Lama has followed the esoteric course, for he has attempted to gain occult and strange powers. His search itself is a "mystical and magic way" of attaining salvation. In the past, "he had been a master hand at casting horoscopes and nativities," occult power he still retains, for he discusses this mysterious science with a Hindu priest.[57] He chants the magic formula "Om Mani Padme Hum," which is usually translated "Hail" (Om), "O Jewel" (Mani), "in the flower of the lotus" (Padme), "Hail" (Hum). The jewel, according to the current interpretation, represents Chen-re-zi, the Dalai Lama, the very incarnation of the Bodhisattva and hence a living Buddha.[58] The Lama has seen the Dalai Lama himself, a unique spiritual and esoteric experience. "He [the Lama] spoke even of Lhassa and of the Dalai Lama, whom he had seen and adored."[59]

The essence of Buddhist teaching is contained in the Four Noble Truths, the Eightfold Path, and the Twelve Causal Connections—the Chain of Causation. As Kim and the Lama wander in India, they attempt to follow the Rule as much as possible:

56 Maraini, *Secret Tibet*, 83.
57 Kipling, *Kim*, 65.
58 Maraini, *Secret Tibet*, 92.
59 Kipling, *Kim*, 349.

So they enjoyed themselves in high felicity, abstaining from evil
words, covetous desires, not over-eating, not lying on high beds,
or wearing rich clothes, as the Rule demands.[60]

The Lama illustrates the two most important paths of the Eightfold Path, Right Mindfulness and Right Concentration. In the incident with the Russian, he was momentarily seized by a passion to
strike back at his opponent. "The Lama rose at the insult; his hand
went to the heavy iron pen-case that is the priest's weapon,"[61]
Instead of meeting evil with Right Mindfulness—the "awareness
of the fundamental truths that every man must always carry with
him"[62]—and reciprocating evil or hate with love—one of the "fundamental Truths"— the Lama is seized by a passionate desire com-
pounded of "anger, rage, and a lust to return evil," for which he
feels repentant later on:

> Had I been passionless, the evil blow would have done only bodily
> evil—a scar, or a bruise—which is illusion. But my mind was not
> abstracted. Rushed in straightway a lust . . . . In fighting that lust,
> my soul was torn and wrenched beyond a thousand blows. Not till
> I had repeated the Blessings (he meant the Buddhist Beatitudes)
> did I achieve calm. But the evil planted in me by that moment's
> carelessness works out its ends. Just is the Wheel, swerving not a
> hair! Learn the lesson, *Chela.*[63]

Hence the mental error he committed resulted in a spiritual wound.
Here the Lama illustrates the inner torment of the Buddhist who
fails to observe the Eightfold Path—in this case, Right Mindfulness.

In ultimately giving up his physical search for the River of Arrow, the Lama follows the last path of the Eightfold Path, Right
Concentration. The purpose of the search was to cleanse himself
of his sins, in order to prepare himself for freedom and Nirvana.
Right Concentration concerns the higher activities of the spirit;
meditation must culminate, by way of various states of ecstasy, in
the abolition of sensibility and consciousness.[64] It was this path that

60 *Ibid.*, 349–50.
61 *Ibid.*, 396.
62 Maraini, *Secret Tibet*, 78.
63 Kipling, *Kim*, 412.
64 Maraini, *Secret Tibet*, 78.

brought the attainment of "Enlightenment" to Buddha. Like Buddha, the Lama prepares himself for Right Meditation in his search:

> I took no food. I drank no water. Still I saw not the Way. . . . So I removed myself to a hollow under a tree. I took no food. I took no water. I sat in meditation two days and two nights, abstracting my mind; upon the second night—so great was my reward—the wise soul loosed itself from the silly body and went free.[65]

This is a unique experience, even to the Lama, who had heard about it but never felt it. Then he describes the "various states of ecstasy," and the flight of the soul to identify its spiritual self with the Universe. This is the relationship between the body as microcosm and the universe as macrocosm, for Truth is not a thing to be learned, but must become an inner physical experience, a trance. Right Concentration and Right Meditation produce the unique experience of seeing into the "Cause of All Things," seeing the reality behind the illusion, a state of mind the Lama describes:

> Yea, my soul went free, and wheeling like an eagle saw indeed that there was no Teshoo Lama nor any other soul. As a drop falls into water, so my soul drew near to the Great Soul which is beyond all things. . . . By this I knew the soul had passed beyond the illusion of Time and Space and of Things. By this I knew that I was free. . . . Also I saw the stupid body of Teshoo Lama lying down. . . . Then my soul was all alone, and I saw nothing, for I was all things, having reached the Great Soul. And I meditated a thousand thousand years, passionless, well aware of the Causes of all Things.[66]

But the Lama cannot completely become a part of the Great Soul. He still has desires, one of them being his attachment to Kim. Thus he reveals that in order to attain Nirvana the true Buddhist must possess complete detachment from all things of the World, which he has not yet achieved. With typical Lamaist symbolism he tells of his return to the body:

> Then a voice cried: "What shall come to the boy if thou art dead?" and I said, "I will return to my *Chela* lest he miss the Way." Upon

[65] Kipling, *Kim*, 471.
[66] *Ibid.*, 472.

this my soul, which is the soul of Teshoo Lama, withdrew itself from the Great Soul with strivings and yearnings and retchings and agonies not to be told. As the egg from the fish, as the fish from the water, as the water from the cloud, as the cloud from the thick air; so put forth, so leaped out, so drew away, so fumed up the soul of Teshoo Lama from the Great Soul.[67]

Kim offers the reader intimate pictures of the education and awareness of a Buddhist priest, personified in the Lama, deeply insistent on following the Law, meeting with obstacles, and attempting to overcome them. In pursuing this course he reflects both the philosophic and aesthetic aspects of Buddhism, of which Kipling reveals much knowledge and deep understanding.

The personality of the Lama and his attitude toward life are presented with reverence, insight and understanding by Kipling, and the other Hindu characters in *Kim* are also drawn in a spirit of tolerance and realism. In Kipling's early short stories we noted his prejudice against the Bengali, and some of the reasons for this feeling. In *Kim*, we encounter another Bengali, Hurree Chunder Mookerjee, the only Hindu character of much importance in the novel. There is a world of difference in the way he is presented as compared to some of Kipling's earlier Bengalis. The main reason for this change in treatment again can be traced to his maturity of mind and new perspective on the Indian synthesis. The sentiments expressed in "The Settler," the poem quoted earlier, were real, and Kipling was permitting them to permeate his last work on India. There is realism, humor, and satire in the presentation of Huree Chunder Mookerjee, but no venomous racial prejudice, as seen in the earlier phase of Kipling's attitude toward the Bengalis.

Hurree Chunder Mookerjee is a great comic creation. The reader laughs with the man, rather than at him, and in his portrait Kipling has set forth some of the eccentricities of the western-educated Indian. Mookerjee has an M.A. degree from Calcutta University, knows French, and speaks English because, as he tells Kim, "All we Babus talk English to show off." He parades his learning before Kim in a clumsy, comical manner:

[67] *Ibid.*

Was Kim going to school? Then he, an M.A. of Calcutta University, would explain the advantages of education. There were marks to be gained by due attention to Latin and Wordsworth's "Excursion" (all this was Greek to Kim). Also a man might go far, as he himself had done, by strict attention to plays called "Lear" and "Julius Caesar," both much in demand by examiners on the Bengal side. "Lear" was not so full of historical allusions as "Julius Caesar," the book cost four annas, but could be bought second-hand in Bow Bazar for two.[68]

His knowledge of Shakespeare consists of interspersing his conversation with quotations from the great bard to prove the most trivial points. To Kim's question, "Why are you here, Babuji?" the Babu replies ponderously, "Ah! *That* is the question as Shakespeare hath said,"[69] and even to the Russian spy with whom he pretends to be friendly, he requests that he be remembered with the parting words of Shakespeare's Othello, "that he, even he, Mohendro Lal Dutt, M.A. of Calcutta, had 'done the state some service.' "[70] When he comes into possession of the secret documents exposing Russia's intention of capturing the northwestern parts of India, he expresses his shock with a Shakespearean phrase, "treason most base . . ." but stops without completing it for he realizes with disappointment that his listener, Kim, cannot understand Shakespeare. "But you do not understand? Eh?"[71] He is also addicted to punning, and makes some very bad ones trying to imitate Shakespeare, "there is no hurry for Hurree," and is satisfied with his coinage, "that is an Europe pun, ha! ha!"[72]

His use of colloquial English idioms is equally humorous, "just you jolly well bet yourself they are,"[73] or "jolly dam quick."[74] He possesses the Indian's deep-rooted fascination with flowery speech. In the language of Hurree Babu, Kipling has exhibited the humor and comedy of the Indian speaking the Queen's English collo-

[68] *Ibid.*, 266.
[69] *Ibid.*, 359.
[70] *Ibid.*, 439.
[71] *Ibid.*, 457.
[72] *Ibid.*, 368.
[73] *Ibid.*, 457.
[74] *Ibid.*, 261.

quially and idiomatically. There is a delightful realism in Babu's speech, for even Indians were aware of the "strangeness" in their newly-acquired foreign language. D. C. Sharma, in an article "The Indians' Use of the English Language" for *The Calcutta Review*, states that during the early days of British Indian universities Indian students tried to speak English like Chaucer and Shakespeare.[75] Hurree Babu is a product of Calcutta University, which was founded in 1857, and therefore represents the "typical English speaking Indian" of those early years.

Hurree Babu is a cog in the wheels of British administration. As a result, he can think or do nothing except from an "official" or "unofficial" or "departmental" point of view. He states that he is not afraid to die, but yet is "fearful of the Russian." His peculiar logic is interesting:

> Oah, thatt is nothing. I am good enough Herbert Spencerian, I trust to meet little thing like death, which is all in my fate, you know. But—but they may beat me.[76]

When Kim quotes a proverb making fun of Hurree Babu's fearfulness, "God made the hare and the Bengali, What shame,"[77] he accepts it by quoting Herbert Spencer:

> It was process of Evolution, I think, from Primal Necessity, but the fact remains in all its *cui bono*. I am, oh, awfully fearful—I remember once they wanted to cut off my head on the road to Lhassa. (No, I've never reached to Lhassa.) I sat down and cried, Mister O'Hara, anticipating Chinese tortures.[78]

Like some of the other Western-educated Indians who think it fashionable to be non-religious, he claims to be an agnostic. He mistakes the Lama's tolerance and courteousness for agnosticism:

> Now it is curious that the old gentleman [the Lama] himself is totally devoid of religiosity. He is not a damn particular . . . . He is pure agnostic in my opinion, same as me.[79]

[75] Diwanchand Sharma, "Indian Writers of English Prose," *Calcutta Review*, Vol. LXVIII (July, 1938), 34.
[76] Kipling, *Kim*, 366.
[77] *Ibid.*
[78] *Ibid.*
[79] *Ibid.*, 297.

Yet he has the Hindu's respect for the holy man, and presents Kim with a silver beetle-leaves-box, because he took care of the "Old Man."

The Babu is comical, but interesting and true to life. He is presented with true sympathetic feeling for the comic spirit, taking his place in the company of a Bottom, a Touchstone, and a Mrs. Malaprop.

In spite of all the eccentricities that make the Babu such a fascinating character, he is serious-minded in his pursuits. He has a scholar's interest in ethnological matters, and utilizes his wanderings in the "great game" to collect information about the customs and manners of hill people. He has contributed scholarly articles to learned journals like *The Asiatic Quarterly Review,* and his great aim in life is to be accepted as a Fellow of the Royal Society, England.

In spite of being "fearful," the Babu is successful in his adventure with the Russian spy. He is a good actor and puts on a convincing show, worthy of a diplomat:

> Under the striped umbrella Hurree Babu was straining ear and brain to follow the quick-poured French, and keeping both eyes on a *kilta* full of maps and documents—an extra large one with a double red oil skin cover. He did not wish to steal anything. He only desired to know what to steal, and, incidentally, how to get away when he had stolen it. He thanked all the Gods of Hindustan, and Herbert Spencer, that there remained some valuables to steal.[80]

He becomes friendly with the Russian with the sole objective of getting the secret papers that spell conspiracy. Lurgan Sahib praises the Babu for his efficiency, a quality Kipling rarely bestowed on an Indian, especially a Bengali:

> From time to time, God causes men to be born . . . who have a lust to go abroad at the risk of their lives and discover news . . . . These men are very few, and of these few, not more than ten are of the best. Among these ten I count the Babu.[81]

Kim is another among the ten, whom "God causes" to be born for

[80] *Ibid.,* 391.
[81] *Ibid.,* 263.

this specific purpose, requiring strength of mind, body, and spirit. Lurgan Sahib, and Kipling through him, equates the Babu to this level. Furthermore, Kim learns from the Babu, becoming, as the Babu puts it, "subordinate to me in an official capacity." This indicates the disappearance of prejudice from Kipling's mind at the time of writing *Kim*.

It may be argued that Kipling praises or presents the Babu in a more favorable light, because he supports the British "game." This does not appear to be valid, in the light of Kipling's early stories. The Bengalis that appear in his short stories "The Head of the District," "The Strange Ride of Morrowbie Jukes," and "His Chance in Life" are by no means anti-British. Grish Chunder De, in "The Head of the District," accepts his responsibilities only to carry out the British law. Yet he is insulted and ridiculed with venomous prejudice. Uncompromising epithets of scorn and satire are heaped on the Bengali in that unfortunate story, "The Enlightenments of Pagett, M.P." In *Kim*, Kipling is at peace with India, both as a man and as a writer. He has graduated from "boy" to "man" in his outlook on India. The reader well may wish that the spirit of this novel had entered Kipling's other writings as well.

Kim is a crowded canvas, and though many of the innumerable characters are not presented in great detail, in their totality they represent the vastness and colorful variety of the Indian scene. There is Mahbub Ali, a Sufi (Free Thinker) by faith, and a rugged Pathan horse dealer from the Indian frontiers. Ali has been drawn with a sureness of touch born out of Kipling's long admiration for these fighting men of the Indian frontiers.

All the diverse castes and races of India are found on the Grand Trunk road, an ever-moving pageant of Indian life, presented in brilliant colors and bold definitions. Kipling briefly touches upon these various people, but they come to light and gain in individuality, just the same. There is the picture of the imperious old Maharanee, the Indian queen, in her

> gaily ornamented *ruth* or family bullock-cart, with a broidered canopy of two domes, like a double-humped camel, which had just

been drawn into the *parao*. Eight men made its retinue, and two of the eight were armed with rusty sabres—sure sign that they followed a person of distinction, for the common folk do not bear arms.[82]

She commands her retinue with dignity and authority, and is generous to the Lama and his *Chela*, Kim.

All classes and strata of Indian society are represented in *Kim*:

The martial Ludhiana Sikh who says, "We do not trouble our heads with doctrine. We fight."[83]

The fat Hindu moneylender, who charges fabulous interest but expresses the sentiment, "It is well to be kind to the poor."[84]

The Amritzar girl with lustrous eyes.

The young soldier of Dogra caste.

The prosperous, but miserly, cultivator and his generous wife.

The *bhistie*, or water carrier, the prototype of Gunga-Din.

The Balti, "some sort of degraded Buddhist" in Mahbub Ali's service.[85]

The old soldier who remembers the 1857 Mutiny.

The Akali, "a wild-eyed, wild haired Sikh devotee in the blue-checked clothes of his faith, with polished-steel quots glistening on the cone of his tall blue turban."[86]

Troops of "long haired, strong scented sansis with baskets of lizards and other unclean food on their backs."[87]

Gangs of *Changars*, "a flat footed, big bosomed, strong limbed, blue petticoated clan of earth carriers."[88]

The seller of Ganges-water.

The "thin-legged, gray bearded Ooryas from down country."[89]

The Letter writer, "a bureau of general misinformation," who wrote a letter for the Lama and signed it "Written by Sobrao Satai,

---

[82] *Ibid.*, 107–108.
[83] *Ibid.*, 48.
[84] *Ibid.*, 47.
[85] *Ibid.*, 32.
[86] *Ibid.*, 101.
[87] *Ibid.*
[88] *Ibid.*, 102.
[89] *Ibid.*, 108.

Failed Entrance Allahabad University, for Venerable Teshoo Lama, the priest of Suchzen looking for a river."[90]

Nowhere else but in Chaucer's "goodlie companie" on their way to Canterbury can we find such variety, humor, and insight into human character as Kipling reveals in his presentation of Indian life on the Grand Trunk Road.

Between the two good novels about India by Englishmen, Kipling's *Kim* and E. M. Forster's *A Passage to India*, *Kim*, achieves much more in effective interpretation of India in terms of permanence and universality than *A Passage to India*.

Written in 1901, much earlier than *A Passage to India*, (1924), *Kim* can still be related to contemporary Indian life. Religion in Indian life, the major theme of *Kim*, is and will continue to be an important influence in shaping the lives of the people of India. Prototypes of Kim, the Hindu street-boy, are a common feature of the Indian street. Holy men, plain and ordinary or devoutly religious like the venerable Teshoo Lama, still wander across the Indian sub-continent in search of peace. There is also a revival of Buddhism in India today, indicated by the many new conversions to that faith and the celebration in India of the 2500th centenary of the Buddha, inaugurated by the Dalai Lama, himself "the Living Buddha." And there is present to an even greater extent in India today "the note of modern progress with old world piety," that Kipling speaks of in *Kim*.[91] Intimately realistic scenes of Indian life are scattered through the novel like frescoes: the India of the outdoors seen in the crowded, bustling, noisy, humorous, and exasperating, but never boring, compartments of the Indian train; the camps by the wayside with their "strange disorder of Asiatic things";[92] the quiet evenings, with holy men sitting under trees and reciting epics or narrating tales with a moral to eager, fascinated groups of people; the colorful Indian bazaars where the sacred cows stroll into the shops, and the not-so-sacred carts roll by; and the snowy hills where the gods of Hindu mythology dwell.

90 *Ibid.*, 171
91 *Ibid.*, 20.
92 *Ibid.*, 106.

All of these are part of present-day India, as they were when *Kim* was written.

A Passage to India hinges on a political question, the Anglo-Indian problem. It is a book with a purpose, that of showing the faults of British rule in India and suggesting a solution—better human relationships between the ruled and the rulers on the personal level. Peter Burra writes in the Everyman's edition of this novel:

> Forster has never deliberately written, like Dickens, a novel with a "Purpose"—an irrelevancy to the dangers of which this art form is particularly exposed—the fact nevertheless remains that *A Passage to India* (1924) is a book which no student of the Indian question can disregard.[93]

The book, however, achieved its purpose in a way different from Forster's suggestion. His hope was for personal relations to improve, and for Indians to be given spiritual citizenship in the Western world. But the conquerors left the land, seeming to agree with the District Collector in *A Passage to India:*

> I have never known anything but disaster result when English people and Indians attempt to be intimate socially. Intercourse, yes. Courtesy by all means. Intimacy—never, never.[94]

The challenge and the opportunity before the British was to make India an extension of the western world, but they failed as completely in using their opportunity as they did in meeting the challenge.

Now that the Anglo-Indian question has been "solved," Forster's work assumes the position of a historical novel. It represents India of the past, however recent that past. Political issues can never have the permanence and universality that the true spirit or religion can, and the essence of India is less in politics than in religion, not sectarianism but the pursuit of a moral, ethical and philosophical approach to human problems.

It is true that the Russian threat between 1850 and 1897 to the

93 London, 1942, p. xlii.
94 Forster, *A Passage to India*, 141.

Northwest of India, with intentions of using it as a springboard for invasion of India, provides a political background in *Kim*. The rapid progress of Russia towards the border of Afghanistan was a cause of alarm and anxiety to the British Government. The Russo-Turkish war of 1877 strained relations between Russia and England, and a war between the two appeared almost inevitable. Furthermore, Russia was seeking ways of infiltration into Indian native states. H. H. Dodwell, writing in *The Cambridge History of India* about the position of the native state in regard to Russian infiltration, states:

> It is in fact highly probable that Russian agents were busy in Kashmir, although they may not have been countenanced by the Maharaja. . . . In 1889 a quantity of correspondence reached the resident by a very questionable channel, implicating the Maharaja in Russian intrigues.[95]

Kipling uses these bits of information to create the backdrop of intrigue and mystery for *Kim*, but the political issue does not dominate the novel, and Kipling does not elaborate on it. The political theme is not paramount in *Kim* as it is in *A Passage to India*.

The northern boundary of India is not completely free, even today, from "foreign" invasion or infiltration. Without going into the present political situation in this part of India, which is much too complicated and not relevant to our study, it can be said that there still exists an atmosphere of mystery and political intrigue by "foreign" agents in this area. *Kim*, therefore, is relevant to present-day India even from that point of view. But it is worth repeating that *Kim*, the least political of Kipling's writings, is his most abiding work on India.

A Passage to India does not convey a satisfactory portrait of India. Forster has shown poor judgment in selecting a Muhammadan character like Dr. Aziz to be the protagonist of a novel intended to interpret India. This does not mean that a Muhammadan cannot be the "hero" of a novel about India; but the nature of

---

[95] H. H. Dodwell, *The Cambridge History of India: The Indian Empire, 1858–1918*, VI, 496.

Forster's theme, which is political and intends to present intrinsic India, does not permit a Muhammadan to be the protagonist because the Muhammadans were as much invaders of India as the British. Trade and commerce brought the British, and religious fanaticism motivated the Muhammadan invasion.

India was invaded by other races as well, the Aryans, the Persians, the Greeks, the Scythians, and others, not to mention the French, the Dutch, the Portuguese and the British. But these invasions, except for the Western ones, which ultimately withdrew from the land, were absorbed into the Indian synthesis. They influenced the native Dravidian culture and, in turn, were influenced. They made for diversity, but never acted to fragment the fundamental unity of India.

The motives and consequences of the Muhammadan invasion were entirely different. Looking upon India as a land of image-worshipers and nonbelievers in the *Koran*, and considering themselves bound by religious duty to convert it to the Islamic faith, the Muhammadan hordes swept into the plains of India.

With their coming, for the first time in Indian history, religious freedom was at stake. Particularly under the Muslim Emperor Aurangzebe (1658–1707), also called "Alamgir," the favorite ruler of Dr. Aziz,[96] the non-Muslims in India suffered great persecution, including imposition of a special religious tax, "Jaziya." Akbar (1542–1605) was the only Muslim ruler who had world vision, and under his administration the non-Muslims of India enjoyed a brief spell of religious toleration. But Akbar, to Dr. Aziz, "was not a true Moslem."[97]

Even Christianity did not bring the alienation that the Muhammadan invasion brought into India. Christian missionaries, some of them, may have been eccentric and narrow-minded, as Kipling represents in "The Judgment of Dungara" or in the personalities of Reverend Mr. Bennett and Father Victor in *Kim*, but they were never guilty of forceful conversion of the non-Christian. It must be said to England's credit that India enjoyed the utmost

[96] Forster, *A Passage to India*, 53.
[97] *Ibid.*, 124.

158

religious freedom under British rule. The Muhammadan, therefore, cannot express the Indian synthesis as the Hindu can. He cannot speak, like Godbole, of the Lord Krishna multiplying himself into innumerable Krishnas and entering all who need him, Muslim, or Hindu, or Christian.

Forster has omitted or failed to recognize an important sector of the Indian community in discussing Indo-British relations in *A Passage to India*. Better personal relationships or being pleasant to each other might have worked with men like Aziz, or Godbole, or the "Show-Indian" Nawab Bahadur, but the crux of Indo-British difficulties lay not so much with these people as in the more important conflict between Indian nationalists and the British administration. The nationalists were not fighting merely for social acceptance, but also for equality in political administration, and more than that, to secure the fundamental right to govern their own country. If Indians were allowed to be political equals, social acceptance would follow, for people would no longer meet as the rulers and the ruled. It was in this nationalist sector that the destiny of India was being forged, not in that sector where there was conflict between associates, the British officials and their Indian subordinates. Failing to mention the "Indian Nationalist" in discussing Indo-British relations, Forster's *A Passage to India* lacks the dimension of completeness. It is not knowledge of India or the gift of interpreting it that has made Forster's novel a classic of the twentieth century, but his literary ability, his aesthetics in the form and technique of novel writing.

If I were asked to name one novel written by an Englishman which genuinely interprets the India of every-day life, the India of the common people, I would unhesitatingly give that honor to Kipling's *Kim*.

VII

Kipling's India from the New Perspective

WHEN KIPLING was twenty-eight years old, there appeared in an English newspaper the following poem about him:

> He knows the slang of silver street, the
>   horrors of Lahore
> And how the man-seal breasts the waves
>   that buffet Labrador.
> He knows the fine gradation 'twixt the
>   General and the Sub,
> And the terms employed by Atkins when
>   they fling him from a pub;
> He knows an Elka's pony's points, the
>   leper's drear abode,
> The seamy side of Simla, the flaring
>   mile-end road;
> He knows the Devil's tone to souls too
>   pitiful to damn;
> He knows the taste of every regimental
>   mess in 'cham';
> He knows enough to annotate the Bible
>   verse by verse;
> And how to draw the shekels from the
>   British public's purse.[1]

This "know-it-all" quality and his seeming readiness to display it is a major element in his writings. Michael Edwardes emphasizes

[1] *Times* (London, February 22, 1894).

this characteristic in "Rudyard Kipling and the Imperial Imagination," an article in *The Twentieth Century:*

> What is the essential quality of Kipling's work? It is, undoubtedly, vulgarity. But not simply of style, for his work is carefully written and uncolloquial. It is the vulgarity of the "Know-all" that characterises his writings. This "Knowingness," the pretence of the completely integrated personality is the key to understand them (his writings).[2]

His "know-all" quality has a definite relationship to the question of Kipling's fidelity to the Indian scene.

In *Something of Myself* he writes that he would sit and listen to the conversations of doctors, engineers and other men in his club with the sole purpose of picking up the technical jargon of various professions in order to incorporate them into a story or poem.[3] In some cases Kipling achieved a happy compromise between factual knowledge and emotional and aesthetic integrity. For example, that great ode to the steam and industrial age, "McAndrew's Hymn," and the use of his clear knowledge of Buddhism and Lamaism in *Kim*. But often he carried his technical knowledge to an extreme, particularly in his last short stories, where he corrupted literary values by cluttering up his writings with accurate facts. Stories like ".007," "The Ship that Found Herself," "Bread upon the Waters," and "The Devil and the Deep Sea" have, for this reason, very little appeal for most readers.

With his Indian tales, Kipling managed successfully to create the illusion that he knew and understood India. His birth in India was regarded by his English readers as an advantage. But it was Kipling the undeveloped boy who lived in India, not the mature man. Even his most sympathetic critics, like Edward Shanks, acknowledge the fact that in his Indian years Kipling lacked significant experience. Shanks writes:

> It sounds perhaps an odd thing to say at this point, but it is nevertheless true that when he left India Kipling's experience was rela-

2 Michael Edwardes, "Rudyard Kipling and the Imperial Imagination," *Twentieth Century*, Vol. CLIII (June, 1953), 422.

3 Kipling, *Something of Myself*, 43.

tively limited. He knew England as a schoolboy knows it, he had known India as a young child and now again as a young journalist.[4]

Another factor was the "I" character that Kipling strengthened and broadened by giving it omniscience and omnipresence. He spoke in the "I," and in his narration developed an intimate tone to establish a personal connection between the reader and himself. He sprinkled his stories with Hindustani words to lend authenticity, and asides—"that's another story"—to indicate the bagful of stories he had. He was brief, and the newness of the material captured his readers, who failed to see the superficiality and glib generalizations inherent in his Indian writings. All these techniques helped to establish him as a fascinating Anglo-Indian storyteller. Moreover, those who read him were not merely being entertained by a clever journalist; they were being influenced to believe in the sanctity of the British Empire, and to think of India in terms of violent prejudices. Kipling, therefore, became a historic political force.

There is no denying Kipling's talents as a technician in the art of storytelling. Kipling is a good storyteller, and no anthology of short stories is complete without including at least one of his works. His stories are technically excellent, with directness of plot, stark simplicity, and narrative movement organized with precision and speed.

It is not easy to judge Kipling separately in two different realms, that of artist in storytelling and that of interpreter and judge of India. To appreciate Kipling's stories, the reader must accept the hypothesis on which they are constructed. A. C. Ward makes this clear in his comments on Kipling in *Aspects of the Modern Short Story*:

> One would wish to speak only of the purely literary qualities of Kipling's work, but the author himself makes such a course almost impossible. Nearly all his Indian stories demand that the reader shall, at the outset grant certain large premises; that the British are God's chosen race; and that in consequence of divine selection, the British can do no wrong. From those initial postulates, Kipling would

[4] *Rudyard Kipling: A Study in Literature and Political Ideas*, 69.

exempt only the few English members of Parliament who occasionally plead the cause of the Indian native, and one or two high officials who similarly offend. Such evidences of racial prejudice cannot easily be set aside in any study of Kipling's work.[5]

"Head of the District" might hold the reader's interest by directness of plot and narration, but the entire story is based upon the assumption that a Bengali is both a fool and a coward, and that a western-trained Indian is a ridiculous specimen. If the reader accepts this premise, then he can appreciate the story. "The Return of Imray," "The Mark of the Beast" and even that most popular story of all, "The Man Who Would Be King," are dependent on the acceptance of the idea that "east of Suez, there aren't no Ten Commandments," and that "the best is like the worst."[6] Only if the reader can accept that "east of Suez" lies a world of uncivilized heathens, can Kipling's Indian tales be appreciated both aesthetically and emotionally.

As George Orwell pointed out, Kipling had sold himself to "the British governing class, not financially but emotionally,"[7] and in turn went out as a super-salesman to convert others to the cause of the empire. Literature became merely a medium for preaching his doctrine, and as Shanks admits in his study, *Rudyard Kipling*, "it would be quite impossible not to make politics a great part of any book about Kipling," for he "adhered to a political doctrine which was the mainspring of his work."[8] His political allegiance was so great that he suppressed his own love for India. None of his writings about India—with the exception of *Kim*—reveals Kipling's deep affection for India. He assumed the role of a political prophet who must sing of the white man's divine role and the white man's burden, and dedicated his writings . . . "To the last and the largest Empire. To the map that is half unrolled!"[9] Kipling's writings with a political flavor are not the ones that reveal his understanding of India. It is his least political work, *Kim*, that captures

5 *Aspects of the Modern Short Story, English and American*, 119.
6 Kipling, "Mandalay," *Rudyard Kipling's Verse*, 417.
7 *Dickens, Dali and Others: Studies in Popular Culture*, 160.
8 *Rudyard Kipling: A Study in Literature and Political Ideas*, 7.
9 "The Native-Born," *Rudyard Kipling's Verse*, 193.

the abiding religious spirit of India, thereby presenting the very heart of the country.

We have examined Kipling's Indian writings in the context of his life, his journalistic qualities, and his political views. Three important facts emerge as a result of this evaluation.

First, Kipling was a local colorist in most of his writings. His life in India was spent mostly in the northern part, where there was a predominant Muslim population and rugged outdoor life was a characteristic feature. Kipling evinces, therefore, great liking for the Muslim character and emphasis on the adventurous life, which particularly suited the galloping rhythm he wanted to capture in some of the Indian ballads. His knowledge of Hindu life was limited, and the life of contemplation finds no expression in his stories until a very late period in his life, when he wrote "The Miracle of Puran Bhagat" and *Kim*.

Second, as a result of his journalistic qualities, which demanded brevity and an odd or abnormal feature in the stories that would make them "stand up," Kipling sacrificed depth of understanding for superficialities, and normal life for sensationalism. His political views as an imperialist and a disbeliever in the democratic process made him contemptuous of the educated Indian who sought an equal share in the administration of his country.

These beliefs led him to glorify the image of the Anglo-Saxon as an empire-builder, an exile, and martyr in a great and divine cause. Glorification of the Anglo-Indian would have been pardonable had it not been for the fact that while doing this Kipling presented India as a cursed land peopled with incompetent Bengalis and weird priests like the Silver man in "The Mark of the Beast." Against this cruel and violent background the Anglo-Indian was expected to assume tragic stature, that of a veritable Prometheus, fighting against "the newly caught sullen people" for the cause of civilization!

Third, it is only in his presentation of the social and official departmental life of the Anglo-Indians, as it revolved around Simla, that Kipling shows true understanding. Here superficiality really existed, and he succeeds in being an authority on it.

Kipling's writings will remain as an authentic answer to one question: How did the staunch, die-hard conservative Englishman react to India? What were his prejudices? To the historian of British rule in India, in its most expansionist phase, Kipling's writings will always represent the attitude of the imperial masters towards colonial India.

What, then, shall be our judgment on Kipling? *Kim*, his last work on India, will influence the verdict. This is his most mature work, written at a time when both his personal life and the life of the empire he believed in were undergoing significant changes. In *Kim*, he comes to terms with himself and asks sincerely, could I have been an Indian in my previous life? Are these external forms merely shadow changing into shadow, a trick of the carcass? Is there no black and white?

The very fact that Kipling questioned and attempted a search of his own indicates his awareness of what was deep and fundamental in Indian life, the knowledge of the Self and its relationship to God, or the Universal Soul. Like Kabir in "A Song of Kabir," which he quotes at the beginning of "The Miracle of Puran Bhagat":

> He has looked upon Man, and his eyeballs are clear—(There was One; there is One; and but One, saith Kabir); The Red Mist of Doing has thinned to a cloud—He has taken the Path . . . .[10]

The mention of Kabir and his philosophic approach is significant, because this mystic, a sixteenth-century Indian reformer, sought to synthesize the best in the Muslim and Hindu faiths. *Kim* expresses the Indian synthesis. It is Kipling's valedictory address to India, and in the light of this, his early writings may be pardoned as the somewhat irresponsible expressions of a self-confident young boy to whom success and fame came too soon. Insight into Indian life came late, in the years of maturity; therefore Kipling must be credited with understanding India, with *Kim* standing solidly as eloquent witness to this fact.

[10] "A Song of Kabir," *ibid.*, 509.

Appendix: Published Works by Kipling Written in India, 1882-1889

The following are the eight books published by Kipling during his stay in India between 1882 and 1889:

"Quartette," *The Christmas Annual of The Civil and Military Gazette.* (1885) This volume contains three prose items by Kipling, one of which "The Unlimited 'DRAW' of 'TICK' Boileau," was uncollected.
Plain Tales From the Hills (1897).

Published in the Indian Railway Library Series:

Soldiers Three. Includes stories from *The Week's News* as late as August 4, 1888.
In Black and White. Includes stories from *The Week's News* as late as August 11, 1888.
The Story of the Gadsbys. Includes stories from *The Week's News* as late as August 18, 1888.
Under the Deodars. Includes stories from *The Week's News* as late as September 8, 1888.
The Phantom Rickshaw. Includes two stories from the 1885 "Quartette," one story from *The Week's News*, February 25, 1888, and the story "The Man Who Would Be King."
Wee Willie Winkie. Includes the story, "The Drums of the Fore and Aft."

The following works were written during Kipling's stay in India, but were published after his departure to England:

The Smith Administration (1891). Includes twenty contributions, sixteen from *The Civil and Military Gazette;* four from *The Pioneer.*

Fourteen short stories, distributed as follows: Ten stories in *Life's Handicap* (1891). One story in certain editions of *The Phantom Rickshaw.* Two stories in some editions of *Plain Tales From the Hills.* One story in *The Day's Work.*

Thirty stories written between February 4, 1888, and February 21, 1890, published as follows: Five stories in *The Week's News.* One story in *The Pioneer.* Twenty-four stories in *The Civil and Military Gazette.*

Bibliography

The Works of Rudyard Kipling

Abaft the Funnel. New York, The B. W. Dodge & Co. (pirated edition), 1909.

Actions and Reactions. New York, Charles Scribner's Sons, 1913.

A Book of Words: Selections from Speeches and Addresses Delivered between 1906–1927. New York, Charles Scribner's Sons, 1928.

The Day's Work. 2 vols. New York, Charles Scribner's Sons, 1899.

Departmental Ditties and Ballads and Barrack-Room Ballads. New York, Doubleday & McClure Company, 1899.

Debits and Credits. New York, Charles Scribner's Sons, 1926.

A Diversity of Creatures. New York, Charles Scribner's Sons, 1917.

Early Verse. New York, Charles Scribner's Sons, 1900.

The Eyes of Asia. Garden City, Doubleday Page, 1918.

The Five Nations. New York, Charles Scribner's Sons, 1913.

From Sea to Sea: Letters of Travel, 1887–1889, 2 vols. New York, Doubleday & McClure, 1899.

Great Kipling Stories: together with a life of Rudyard Kipling by Lowell Thomas. Philadelphia, J. C. Winston, 1936.

In Black and White. New York, Charles Scribner's Sons, 1897.

The Irish Guards in the Great War. New York, Charles Scribner's Son's 1923.

The Jungle Book. New York, Charles Scribner's Sons, 1897.

The Second Jungle Book. New York, Charles Scribner's Sons, 1897.

Just So Stories for Little Children. New York, Doubleday, Page & Company, 1902.

Kim. New York, Charles Scribner's Sons, 1916.

Land and Sea Tales for Boys and Girls. New York, Charles Scribner's Sons, 1937.

Letters of Travel: 1892–1913. New York, Charles Scribner's Sons, 1920.

Life's Handicap. Garden City, Doubleday, Page, 1923.

The Light That Failed. New York, Charles Scribner's Sons, 1913.

Many Inventions. New York, D. Appleton and Co., 1899.

Mine Own People. Philadelphia, Henry T. Coates, 1890.

Naulahka: A Story of West and East. New York, Charles Scribner's Sons, 1897.

"On the Manufacture of Indian Anarchists," *Spectator*, Vol. CIV (March 19–26, 1910), 459–60, 504.

The Phantom Rickshaw and Other Stories. Philadelphia, Altemus, 1898.

Plain Tales from the Hills. New York, Charles Scribner's Sons, 1916.

The Puck of Pook's Hill. New York, Charles Scribner's Sons, 1913.

Rewards and Fairies. New York, Charles Scribner's Sons, 1916.

Rudyard Kipling's Verse (Definitive Edition). New York, Doubleday Doran & Co., Inc., 1945.

Soldiers Three and Other Military Tales. 2 vols. New York, Charles Scribner's Sons, 1898.

Something of Myself, For My Friends Known and Unknown. Garden City, Doubleday, Doran & Co., Inc., 1937.

Stalky and Co. New York, Charles Scribner's Sons, 1916.

Traffics and Discoveries. New York, Charles Scribner's Sons, 1913.

Under the Deodars: The Story of the Gadsbys; Wee Willie Winkie. New York, Charles Scribner's Sons, 1916.

War Writings and Poems. New York, Charles Scribner's Sons, 1937.

The Years Between and Poems From History. New York, Charles Scribner's Sons, 1919.

Books

Adams, Francis. *Essays in Modernity*. London, John Lane, 1899.

Archer, William. *Poets of the Younger Generation*. London, John Lane, 1902.

Arnold, Sir Edwin. *The Light of Asia*. Boston, Roberts Brothers, 1880.

Arnold, William Delafield. *Oakfield or Fellowship in the East*. 2 vols. London, Longmans, Green, 1854.

Around the World with Kipling. Garden City, Doubleday, Page, 1926.

Auden, Wystan Hugh. *Collected Poems*. New York, Random House, 1945.

Baker, Sir Herbert. *Cecil Rhodes*. London, Oxford University Press, 1934.

Baker, Joseph E., ed. *The Reinterpretation of Victorian Literature*. Princeton, Princeton University Press, 1950.

Balestier, Wolcott. *The Average Woman and Other Stories*. London, William Heinemann, 1892.

Basham, Arthur Llewellyn. *The Wonder That Was India*. London, Sedgwick & Jackson, 1954.

Beerbohm, Max. *A Christmas Garland*. London, William Heinemann, 1912.

Bennett, Arnold. *Books and Persons: Being Comments on a Past Epoch*. New York, George H. Doran, 1917.

Bentley, Eric, ed. *The Importance of Scrutiny*. New York, George W. Stewart, 1948.

Beresford, G. C. *Schooldays With Kipling*. New York, G. P. Putnam & Sons, 1936.

Besant, Sir Walter. *All in a Garden Fair: The Simple Story of Three Boys and a Girl*. London, Chatto & Windus, 1883.

Blunt, Wilfrid Scawen. *My Diaries: Being a Personal Narrative of Events, 1888–1914*. 2 vols. New York, Alfred A. Knopf, 1921.

Bose, Sudhindra. *Some Aspects of British Rule in India*. Iowa City, University Press, 1916.

Braddy, Nella. *Rudyard Kipling: Son of Empire*. New York, Messner, 1942.

Braybrooke, Patrick. *Kipling and His Soldiers*. Philadelphia, J. B. Lippincott, 1925.

———. *Philosophies in Modern Fiction*. London, C. W. Daniel Co., 1929.

Bridges, Robert. *Collected Essays and Papers*. Vol. II. London, Oxford University Press, 1933.

Brinda, Maharani of Kapurthala. *Maharani: The Story of an Indian Princess*, as told to Elaine Williams. New York, Henry Holt, 1954.

Brinton, Crane. *English Political Thought in the Nineteenth Century*. London, E. Benn, 1933.

Bromfield, Louis. *The Rains Came*. New York, Harpers, 1937.

Brown, Hilton, *Rudyard Kipling*. New York, Harpers, 1945.

Buck, Sir Edward John. *Simla, Past and Present*. 2nd edition. Bombay, Times Press, 1925.

Canby, Henry Seidel. *A Study of the Short Story*. New York, Henry Holt, 1935.

Carpenter, W. M. *A Few Significant and Important Kipling Items*. Evanston, Illinois, Alderbrink Press, 1930.

Carrington, Charles E. *The Life of Rudyard Kipling*. Garden City, Doubleday, 1955.

Carstairs, Robert. *The Little World of an Indian District Officer*. London, Macmillan & Co., 1912.

Catalogue of English and American Authors. New York, American Art Association, 1928.

Chandler, Lloyd Horwitz. *A Summary of the Works of Rudyard Kipling*. New York, The Grolier Club, 1930.

Chesney, Sir George Tomkyns. *A True Reformer*. 3 vols. London, G. P. Putnam & Sons, 1873.

Chesterton, Gilbert Keith. *Heretics*. New York, Dodd, Mead, 1923.

———. *The Victorian Age in Literature*. London, Henry Holt, 1913.

Chevrillon, André. *Three Studies in English Literature: Kipling, Galsworthy, Shakespeare,* Translated by Florence Simmonds. New York, Doubleday, Page, 1923.

[Clarke, William James]. G. F. Monkshood (pseud.). *Less Familiar Kipling and Kiplingiana.* London, Jarrolds, 1936.

———. *Rudyard Kipling, the Man and His Work: An Attempt at Appreciation.* London, Greening, 1902.

Clemens, William. *A Ken of Kipling.* New York, New Amsterdam Book Co., 1899.

Clemens, Samuel. *The Adventures of Tom Sawyer.* New York, Heritage Press, 1936.

Conrad, Joseph. *The Nigger of the "Narcissus," a Tale of the Sea.* With an introduction by Morton Dauwen Zabel. New York, Harpers, 1951.

Crawford, F. Marion. *Mr. Isaacs, a Tale of Modern India.* New York, Macmillan & Co., 1931.

Crescent and Green: A Miscellany of Writings on Pakistan. London, Cassel & Co., 1955.

Croft-Cooke, Rupert. *Rudyard Kipling.* London, Home & Van Thal Ltd., 1948.

Crooke, William. *The North-Western Provinces of India, Their History and Administration.* London, Methuen, 1897.

The Cultural Heritage of India: Sri Rama Krishna Centenary Memorial. 3 vols. Calcutta, Sri Rama Krishna Centenary Committee, [1936?].

Cunliffe, John William. *English Literature During the Last Half-Century.* New York, Macmillan & Co., 1919.

Cunningham, Henry S. *Chronicles of Dustypore: A Tale of Modern Anglo-Indian Society.* London, Smith, Elder & Co., 1875.

Cushing, Harvey. *The Life of Sir William Osler.* Oxford, Oxford University Press, 1925.

Davids, Rhys T. W. (trans.). *Buddhist Birth Stories or Jataka Tales.* London, K. Paul, Trench, Trübner & Co., 1880.

Davitt, Michael. *The Boer Fight for Freedom.* New York, Funk & Wagnalls, 1902.

Dobrée, Bonamy. *The Lamp and the Lute, Studies in Six Modern Authors*. Oxford, Clarendon Press, 1929.

———. *Modern Prose Style*. Oxford, Clarendon Press, 1934.

Dodwell, H. H. (ed.). *The Cambridge History of India: The Indian Empire, 1858–1918*. Vol. VI. New York, Macmillan, 1932.

Doyle, Arthur Conan. *Memories and Adventures*. Boston, Little, Brown & Co., 1924.

Dufferin and Ava, Frederick Hamilton-Temple-Blackwood, Marquis of. *Speeches Delivered in India, 1884–8*. London, John Murray, 1890.

Dufferin and Ava, Hariot Georgina Hamilton-Temple-Blackwood, Marchioness of. *Our Viceregal Life in India: Selections From My Journal, 1884–88*. New York, Scribner & Welford, 1890.

Dunbar, Janet. *Golden Interlude: The Edens in India 1836–1842*. London, John Murray, 1955.

Dunsterville, Lionel Charles. *More Yarns by "Stalky."* London, Jarrolds, 1931.

Dunsterville, Lionel Charles. *Stalky's Adventures*. London, Jonathan Cape, 1933.

———. *Stalky's Reminiscences*. London, Jonathan Cape, 1928.

Durand, Sir Henry Mortimer. *Life of The Right Honourable Sir Alfred Comyn Lyall*. Edinburgh, William Blackwood, 1913.

Durand, Ralph. *A Handbook to the Poetry of Rudyard Kipling*. Garden City, Doubleday, Page, 1914.

Dutt, Romesh Chunder. *The Economic History of India in the Victorian Age: From the Accession of Queen Victoria in 1837 to the Commencement of the Twentieth Century*. London, Kegan Paul, 1908.

Eliot, T. S. *A Choice of Kipling's Verse*. New York, Charles Scribner's Sons, 1943.

Elsmie, George Robert. *Thirty-Five Years in the Punjab, 1858–1893*. Edinburgh, D. Douglas, 1908.

English Association, The United Provinces Branch. *Essays and Studies*. Allahabad, Indian Press, 1938.

Falls, Cyril. *Rudyard Kipling: A Critical Study*. New York, Mitchell Kennerley, 1915.

Fay, Mrs. Eliza. *Original Letters from India*. Introduction by E. M. Forster. New York, Harcourt, Brace, 1925.

Forster, Edward Morgan. *Abinger Harvest*. New York, Harcourt, Brace, 1936.

——. *The Hill of Devi*. New York, Harcourt, Brace, 1953.

——. *A Passage to India*. With an introduction by Peter Burra and notes by the author. London, J. M. Dent, 1942.

Frazer, R. W. *A Literary History of India*. New York, Charles Scribner's Sons. 1898.

Furnivall, John S. *Colonial Policy and Practice: A Comparative Study of Burma and Netherlands India*. New York, New York University Press, 1956.

Gandhi, Mohandas Karamchand. *The Story of My Experiments with Truth*. Washington, D.C., Public Affairs Press, 1948.

Garland, Hamlin. *My Friendly Contemporaries*. New York, Macmillan & Co., 1932.

——. *Roadside Meetings*. New York, Macmillan, 1930.

Gladstone, W. Ewert. *Gleanings of Past Years, 1843–78*. New York, Charles Scribner's Sons, 1879.

Gosse, Edmund. *Questions At Issue*. New York, William Heinemann, 1893.

Griffiths, Sir Percival Joseph. *The British Impact on India*. London, Macdonald, 1952.

Grolier Club. *Catalogue of the Works of Rudyard Kipling*. New York, The Grolier Club, 1930.

Gunther, John. *Inside Asia*. New York, Harpers, 1939.

Harrer, Heinrich, *Seven Years in Tibet*. Translated by Richard Graves. New York, E. P. Dutton, 1954.

Harris, Frank. *Contemporary Portraits*. Vol. 2, Second Series. New York, Mitchell Kennerley, 1915.

Hart, Walter Morris. *Kipling, the Story Writer*. Berkeley, University of California Press, 1918.

Harte, Bret. *Condensed Novels: New Burlesques*. Second Series. New York, Houghton Mifflin, 1902.

Hearn, Lafcadio. *A History of English Literature*. Vol. II. Tokyo, Hokuseido Press, 1927.

——. *Japanese Letters*. Edited, with an introduction, by Elizabeth Bisland. Boston, Houghton Mifflin, 1910.

Hicks, Granville. *Figures in Transition: A Study of British Literature at the End of the Nineteenth Century*. New York, Macmillan, 1939.

Hobson, John Atkinson. *The War in South Africa: Its Causes and Effects*. London, Macmillan, 1900.

——. *The Psychology of Jingoism*. London, G. Richards, 1901.

Hollis, Christopher. *A Study of George Orwell: The Man and His Works*. Chicago, Henry Regnery, 1956.

Hopkins, R. Thurston. *Rudyard Kipling: A Literary Appreciation*. New York, Frederick A. Stokes, 1915.

——. *A Survey of His Literary Art*. London, Digby, Long & Co., 1914.

——. *Rudyard Kipling: A Character Study, Life, Writings and literary landmarks*. London, Simpkin, 1927.

Hubbard's Newspaper and Bank Directory of the World. 2 vols. New Haven, Connecticut, H. P. Hubbard, 1882.

Hunter, William Wilson. *The Imperial Gazetteer of India*. London, K. Paul, Trübner, Trench, 1881.

Jackson, Holbrook. *The Eighteen Nineties: A View of Art and Ideas at the Close of the Nineteenth Century*. New York, Alfred A. Knopf., 1922.

James, Henry. Introduction to Rudyard Kipling's *Mine Own People*, and *Black and White*. Philadelphia, Wanamaker, 1898.

——. *Views and Reviews*. Boston, Ball Publishing Co., 1908.

——. *Letters*. Selected and Edited by Percy Lubbock. 2 vols. New York, Charles Scribner's Sons, 1920.

——. *Henry James and Robert Louis Stevenson: A Record of Friendship and Criticism*. Edited, with an introduction, by Janet Adam Smith. London, Rupert Hart-Davis, 1948.

Johnson, Lionel Pigot. *Reviews and Critical Papers*. New York, E. P. Dutton, 1921.

Kernham, Coulson. *Six Famous Living Poets*. London, Butterworth, 1922.

Kincaid, Dennis. *British Social Life in India, 1608–1937*. London, G. Routledge & Sons, 1938.

The Kipling Index: Being a Guide to the Uniform and Pocket Editions of Rudyard Kipling's Works. London, Macmillan, 1914.

Kipling, John Lockwood. *Beast and Man in India: A Popular Sketch of Indian Animals in their Relations With the People*. London, Macmillan, 1891.

The Kipling Journal, issued by The Kipling Society, London, 1927–1956.

Knowles, Frederick Lawrence. *A Kipling Primer*. Boston, Little, Brown, 1899.

Korbel, Josef. *Danger in Kashmir*. Princeton, Princeton University Press, 1954.

Le Gallienne, Richard. *Rudyard Kipling: A Criticism*. With a bibliography by John Lane. London, John Lane, 1900.

Landor, Henry Savage. *Tibet and Nepal*. London, A. & C. Black, 1905.

Langer, William L. *The Diplomacy of Imperialism: 1890–1902*. 2nd edition. New York, Alfred A. Knopf, 1951.

Lawrence, Sir Walter Roper. *The India We Serve*. With an introductory letter by Rudyard Kipling. London, Cassell, 1928.

Lawton, William Cranston. *Rudyard Kipling, the Artist: A Retrospect and a Prophecy*. New York, Morse, 1899.

Livingston, Flora V. *Bibliography of the Works of Rudyard Kipling*. New York, Edgar H. Wells, 1927.

———. *Supplement to Bibliography of the Works of Rudyard Kipling*. Cambridge, Harvard University Press, 1938.

Lyall, Sir Alfred Comyn. *The Life of the Marquis of Dufferin and Ava*. 2 vols. London, John Murray, 1905.

———. *Studies in Literature and History*. London, John Murray, 1915.

Lynd, Robert. *Old and New Masters*. London, George Allen & Unwin, 1919.

Macaulay, Thomas Babington. *Essays on Lord Clive and Warren Hastings*. Boston, Houghton Mifflin, 1910.

MacMunn, Sir George Fletcher. *Kipling's Women*. London, S. Low, Marston, 1933.

———. *Rudyard Kipling: Craftsman*. London, R. Hale, 1937.

Mansfield, Milburg Francisco and A. Wessels. *Kiplingiana*. New York, Mansfield & Wessels, 1899.

Maraini, Fosco. *Secret Tibet*. New York, The Viking Press, 1952.

Martindell, Ernest W. *Bibliography of the Works of Rudyard Kipling*, 1881–1923. London, John Lane, 1923.

Masters, John. *Bhowani Junction*. New York, The Viking Press, 1954.

———. *Bugles and a Tiger: A Volume of Autobiography*. New York, The Viking Press, 1956.

———. *Coromandel!* New York, The Viking Press, 1955.

———. *The Deceivers*. New York, The Viking Press, 1952.

———. *The Lotus and the Wind*. New York, The Viking Press, 1953.

———. *Night Runners of Bengal*. New York, The Viking Press, 1951.

Matthews, Brander. *Aspects of Fiction*. New York, Harpers, 1896.

Maugham, Somerset. *The Razor's Edge*. Philadelphia, Blakiston Co., 1945.

———. *A Writer's Notebook*. Garden City, Doubleday, Page, 1949.

———. *Maugham's Choice of Kipling's Best*. Garden City, Doubleday, Page, 1953.

Maurois, André. *Poets and Prophets*. London, Miles, 1936.

Mayo, Katharine. *Mother India*. New York, Harcourt, Brace, 1927.

Mazumdar, Ramesh C., and Others, *An Advanced History of India*. 3 vols. London, 1949.

Migot, André. *Tibetan Marches*. Translated by Peter Fleming. New York, E. P. Dutton, 1955.

Mookherjee, Radhakumud. *The Fundamental Unity of India from Historical Sources*. London, Longmans, Green, 1914.

Moore, George. *Avowals.* New York, William Heinemann, 1926.

More, Paul Elmer. *Shelburne Essays, Second Series.* New York, Putnam, 1907.

Morgan, W. Kenneth (ed.). *The Path of the Buddha: Buddhism Interpreted by Buddhists.* New York, The Ronald Press, 1956.

Mott, Frank Luther. *Golden Multitudes: The Story of the Best-Sellers in the United States.* New York, Macmillan, 1947.

Muddiman, Bernard. *The Men of the Nineties.* London, H. Danielson, 1920.

Muhammad Latif, Saiyid, Khan Bahadur. *Lahore: Its History, Architectural Remains and Antiquities, with an Account of Its Modern Institutions, Inhabitants, their Trade, Customs, Etc.* Lahore, New Imperial Press, 1892.

Munson, Arley. *Kipling's India.* Garden City, Doubleday, Page, 1915.

Nicolls, Beverley. *Verdict on India.* New York, Harpers, 1927.

Nicolls, W. R., and T. J. Wise. *Literary Anecdotes of the Nineteenth Century.* London, Hodder & Stoughton, 1896.

Oaten, Edward Farley. *A Sketch of Anglo-Indian Literature.* London, Kegan Paul, 1908.

Orwell, George. *Burmese Days.* New York, Harpers, 1934.

———. *Dickens, Dali, and Others: Studies in Popular Culture.* New York, Reynal & Hitchcock, 1946.

Paine, Albert Bigelow. *Mark Twain: A Biography.* New York, Harpers, 1912.

Palmer, John Leslie. *Rudyard Kipling.* London, Nisbett, 1915.

Panikkar, Sirdar K. M. *An Introduction to the Study of the Relations of Indian States with the Government of India.* London, Martin Hopkins, 1927.

Parker, William B. *The Religion of Mr. Kipling.* New York, M. F. Mansfield & A. Wessels, 1899.

Pearson, Hesketh. *The Whispering Gallery: Being Leaves from the Diary of an Ex-Diplomat.* New York, Boni & Liveright, 1926.

Peddicord, W. J. *Rudyard Reviewed: A Review of Rudyard Kipling's "American Notes."* Portland, Oregon, Marsh Printing Co., 1900.

Perry, Bliss. *And Gladly Teach—Reminiscences.* Boston, Houghton Mifflin, 1935.

Phelps, William Lyon. *Essays on Modern Novelists.* New York, Macmillan, 1926.

Quennell, Peter. *The Singular Preference: Portraits and Essays.* London, Collins, 1952.

Radhakrishnan, Sarvepalli. *Religion and Society.* London, George Allen & Unwin, 1947.

Ralph, Julian. *War's Brighter Side.* London, C. A. Pearson, 1901.

Rao, G. Subba. *Indian Words in English: A Study in Indo-British Cultural Relations.* Oxford, Clarendon Press, 1954.

Ray, Gordon N. *Thackeray, the Uses of Adversity, 1811–1846.* New York, McGraw-Hill, 1955.

Ray, Prithwis Chandra. *Life and Times of C. R. Das: The Story of Bengal's Self-Expression.* London, Oxford University Press, 1927.

Rice, Howard C. *Rudyard Kipling in New England.* Brattleboro, Vermont, Stephen Daye Press, 1936.

Rideing, William H. *The Boyhood of Famous Authors.* New York, Crowell, 1897.

Rickword, Edgell (ed.). *Scrutinies.* London, Wishart, 1928.

Robertson, John Henry. *W. E. Henley.* London, Constable, 1949.

Rodenbough, F. Theo. *Afghanistan and the Anglo-Russian Dispute.* London, Putnam, 1885.

Sanderson, Gorham D. *India and British Imperialism.* New York, Bookman Associates, 1951.

Saunders, Kenneth. *The Heritage of Asia.* Calcutta, Association Press, 1956.

Scott, W. Dixon. *Men of Letters.* London, Hodder & Stoughton, 1916.

Scott, Walter. *The Surgeon's Daughter.* New York, George Routledge, 1831.

Sencourt, Robert. *India in English Literature.* London, Simpkin, 1923.

Shanks, Edward. *Rudyard Kipling, A Study in Literature and Political Ideas.* New York, Doubleday, Doran, 1940.

179

————. *Second Essays on Literature*. London, Collins, 1927.

Shen, Tsung-Lien. *Tibet and the Tibetans*. Stanford, California, Stanford University Press, 1952.

Sheridan, Clare. *West and East*. New York, Boni & Liveright, 1923.

Singh, Bhupal. *A Survey of Anglo-Indian Fiction*. London, Oxford University Press, 1934.

Sitaramayya, Pattabhi. *History of the Indian National Congress*. 2 vols. Madras, Padma Publications, 1935.

Somervell, David Churchill. *English Thought in the Nineteenth Century*. New York, Longmans, Green, 1929.

Spencer, Walter Thomas. *Forty Years in My Bookshop*. Boston, Houghton Mifflin, 1923.

Steel, Flora Annie. *Garden of Fidelity: An Autobiography*. London, Macmillan, 1929.

Stevenson, Robert Louis. *Letters*. Edited by Sidney Colvin. New York, Charles Scribner's Sons, 1911.

Sunderland, Jabez T. *India in Bondage: Her Right to Freedom and a Place among the Great Nations*. New York, Lewis Copeland, 1932.

Tagore, Rabindranath. *Gora*. London, Macmillan, 1925.

Tapp, Major H. A. *The United Services College, 1874–1911*. Portsmouth, Gale & Polden, 1933.

Taylor, Meadows. *Tara, a Mahratta Tale*. 3 vols. Edinburgh, Blackwood, 1863.

Tennyson, Hallam. *India's Walking Saint: The Story of Vinobha Bhave*. Garden City, Doubleday, Page, 1955.

Thirkell, Angela. *Three Houses*. London, Oxford University Press, 1931.

Thompson, Edward. *The Making of Modern Princes*. London, Oxford University Press, 1943.

The Memoirs of Samuel Foote. Ed. by William Cooke. 3 vols. London, Richard Phillips, 1805.

The Times, London. Fifty Years: Memories and Contrasts: a Composite Picture of the Period, 1882–1932. With a foreword by George Macaulay Trevelyan. London, Butterworth, 1932.

Tindall, William York. *Forces in Modern British Literature*, 1885–1946. New York, Alfred A. Knopf, 1947.

Todd, James. *Annals and Antiquities of Rajastahan, the Central and Western Rajpoot States of India*. 2 vols. New York, E. P. Dutton, 1914.

Trilling, Lionel. *The Liberal Imagination*. New York, The Viking Press, 1951.

Useem, John and Ruth Hill. *The Western Educated Man in India: A Study of his Social Roles and Influences*. New York, Dryden Press, 1955.

Van De Water, Frederic F. *Rudyard Kipling's Vermont Feud*. New York, Reynal & Hitchcock, 1937.

Walker, Hugh. *The Literature of the Victorian Era*. Cambridge University Press, 1910.

Ward, Alfred C. *Aspects of the Modern Short Story, English and American*. London, University of London Press, 1924.

Waugh, Alec. *Island in the Sun*. New York, Farrar, Strauss & Cudahy, 1955.

Wells, Herbert George. *Experiment in Autobiography: Discoveries and Conclusions of a Very Ordinary Brain (Since 1866)*. 2 vols. New York, Macmillan, 1934.

Weygandt, Ann Matlack. *Kipling's Reading and Its Influence on His Poetry*. Philadelphia, University of Pennsylvania Press, 1939.

Wheeler, Stephen. *The Ameer Abdur Rahman*. London, Bliss, Sands & Foster, 1895.

Whyte, Frederic. *William Heinemann, a Memoir*. Garden City, Doubleday, Doran, 1929.

Williams, Jesse Lynch. *Rudyard Kipling*. New York, Charles Scribner's Sons, 1899.

Wilson, Edmund. *The Wound and the Bow*. Boston, Houghton Mifflin, 1941.

Wingfield-Stratford, Esme, Cecil. *The Foundations of British Patriotism*. London, G. Routledge, 1939.

Wolfe, Theodore F. *Literary Haunts and Homes, American Authors*. Philadelphia, Lippincott, 1899.

Worster, W. *Merlin's Isle: A Study of Rudyard Kipling's England.* London, Gyldendal, 1911.

Yeats-Brown, Francis. *The Lives of a Bengal Lancer.* New York, The Viking Press, 1930.

Young, W. Arthur. *A Dictionary of the Characters and Scenes in the Stories and Poems of Rudyard Kipling, 1886–1911.* London, G. Routledge, 1911.

Young, George Malcolm. *Stanley Baldwin.* London, R. Hart-Davis, 1952.

Articles

Babbitt, Irving. "Romanticism and the Orient," *Bookman*, Vol. LXXIV (December, 1931), 352–54.

Barkham, John. "At the Heart of A Dawning World" (a review of *Bhowani Junction* by John Masters), *New York Times Book Review*, March 28, 1954.

Barrie, Sir James M. "Mr. Kipling's Stories," *Contemporary Review*, Vol. LIX (March, 1891), 364–72.

Benson, Mary. "Reminiscences of the Kipling Family," *Sunday Magazine*, Vol. XXVIII (December, 1899), 822–26.

Bhattacharjee, Mohinimohan. "Rudyard Kipling: An Appreciation," *Calcutta Review*, Vol. LIX (April–May, 1936), 97–106, 177–89.

Birkenhead, Earl of. "The Young Rudyard Kipling," *Transactions of the Royal Society of Literature*, Vol. XXVII (1955), 65–88.

Brady, Thomas F. "The Eighty Years of Mr. Maugham," *New York Times Magazine* (January 24, 1954), 12, 52–54.

Chaudhuri, Nirad C. "Passage to and From India," *Encounter*, Vol. II (June, 1954), 19–24.

Collins, J. P. "Rudyard Kipling at Lahore," *Nineteenth Century and After*, Vol. CXXI (January, 1937), 80–90.

Crawford, F. Marion. "The Press in India," *New York Daily Tribune*, March 11, 1883, p. 3.

Edwardes, Michael. "Rudyard Kipling and the Imperial Imagination," *Twentieth Century*, Vol. CLIII (June, 1953), 443–54.

Forbes, Edgar Allen. "Across India with Kim," *World's Work*, Vol. XXIV (October, 1912), 639–49.

"The Horror Tales of Mr. Kipling," *Bookman*, Vol. XII (December, 1900), 330.

"The Indian Mutiny in Fiction," *Blackwood's Magazine*, Vol. CLXI (February, 1897), 231.

"Indian Student, An." "Kipling's Conception of India," *Lippincott's Monthly Magazine*, Vol. XCIV (August, 1914), 177–85.

"Kipling's Return to India," *Bookman*, Vol. I (June, 1885), 291.

Krishnaswami, P. R. "Indian Characters in English Fiction," *Empire Review* (London), Vol. XLIII (January, 1926), 34–40.

MacMunn, Sir George Fletcher. "Some Kipling Origins," *Blackwood's Magazine*, Vol. CCXXII (August, 1927), 145–54.

———. "Some Origins of Kipling's Stories," *India*, Vol. I (August, 1928), 21–23, 38.

Miller, Betty Bergson. "Kipling's First Novel," *Cornhill Magazine*, Vol. CLXXII (Spring, 1956), 405–12.

Montgomery, M. "The Nationality of Kipling's *Kim*," *Germanische-Romanische Monatschrift*, Vol. VI (October–November, 1914), 587–88.

Norton, Charles Eliot. "The Poetry of Rudyard Kipling," *Atlantic*, Vol. LXXIX (January, 1897), 111–15.

Packard, Winthrop. "Rudyard Kipling: An Estimate," *National Magazine*, Vol. X (April, 1899), 77–79.

Power, William R. "Uncollected Kipling Items," *Notes and Queries*, 12th series, Vol. VII (August 14, 1920), 136.

Robinson, E. Kay. "Kipling in India," *McClure's*, Vol. VII (July, 1896), 99–109.

———. "Mr. Kipling as a Journalist," *Academy* (London), Vol. IV (March 18, 1899), 284–86.

Roosevelt, Theodore. "A Colonial Survival," *Cosmopolitan*, Vol. XIV (December, 1892), 229–36.

Roy, Sarath A. R. "Rudyard Kipling Seen Through Hindu Eyes," *North American Review*, Vol. CXCIX (February, 1914), 271–81.

Sharma, Diwanchand. "Indian Writers of English Prose," *Calcutta Review*, Series 3, Vol. LXVIII (July, 1938), 33–50.

Singh, Nihal. Indians and Anglo-Indians: As Portrayed to Britons by British Novelists," *Modern Review*, Vol. XXXVI (September, 1924), 251–56.

Stevenson, Lionel. "The Ideas in Kipling's Poetry," *University of Toronto Quarterly*, Vol. I (July, 1932), 467–89.

Stoddard, Charles Warren. "Rudyard Kipling at Naulahka," *National Magazine*, Vol. XXII (June, 1905), 259–68.

Thompson, C. Patrick. "The White-faced Boy of Lahore," *World Review*, Vol. VIII (February 25, 1929), 56–57.

Varley, Henry Leland. "Imperialism and Rudyard Kipling," *Journal of the History of Ideas*, Vol. XIV (January, 1953), 124–35.

Waterhouse, Francis Asbury. "The Literary Fortunes of Kipling," *Yale Review*, Vol. X (July, 1912), 817–31.

Woolcott, Alexander. "Shouts and Murmurs," *The New Yorker*, Vol. VI (September 13, 1930), 38.

Unpublished Material

Brown, E. I. "Burma and Kipling." Unpublished Master's thesis, University of Southern California, 1926.

Buckland, Roscoe L. "Anglo Saxonism in America, 1880–1898." Ph.D. dissertation, State University of Iowa, 1955. Ann Arbor Michigan, University Microfilms, 1955.

Campbell, Bertha Belle. "Kipling's Women." Unpublished Master's thesis, State University of Iowa, 1919.

Faithe, Richardson. "Kipling's Types of Indian Characters." Unpublished Master's thesis, University of Colorado, 1932.

Ray, Bessie L. "Kipling's Pictures of the Relation of the Two Races in India." Unpublished Master's essay, Columbia University, 1931.

Varley, Henry Leland. "A Study in the Career of Rudyard Kipling." Unpublished Ph.D. dissertation, University of Wisconsin, 1953.

Index

Abolition of Slavery in India
   (1883): 29
Andrews, C. F.: 51
"Anglicists," conflict of with
   "Orientalists": 28
Anglo-Indian: 9, 12, 43, 44, 49,
   55, 67, 87–88; writers, 9–10, 45;
   melancholy of, 52–54; women,
   67–70
Anglo-Saxon myth: 5, 10, 13, 14,
   36
Arms Act: 29, 57
Arnold, Edwin: 45
Arnold, W. D. (Anglo-Indian
   novelist): 45
Auden, W. H.: 42

Baldwin, Alfred: 18
Balestier, Wolcott: 34, 102–120
Bengal: 93
Bentham, Jeremy: 93
Bentinck, Lord William: 93
Besant, Walter: 32
Bhattacharjee, M. M.: 8
Bhave: 137
Blunt, W. S.: 20
Bose, Jagadish Chandra: 93

Brady, Thomas F.: 41
Brinda, Princess: 105
British soldier in India: 71
Brown, Hilton: 7
Buddhism: 145, 146, 148, 155; in
   Kim, 132–33, 135, 141, 142, 149
Burke, Edmund: 9, 76
Burne-Jones, Sir Edward: 18
Burra, Peter: 156

Calcutta Review: 27
Carrington, C. E.: 31, 32, 71, 72
Catholic Emancipation Act
   (1829): 29
Chamberlain, Joseph: 5
Charter Act of 1853: 93
Chaudhuri, Nirad C.: 10
Chesney, George M., Jr.: 51,
   57–59, 61–62
Civil and Military Gazette: 5, 24,
   25, 27, 30, 31, 42, 64
Clive, Lord: 9, 44
Colonialism: *see* Imperialism
Conrad, Joseph: 59
Cunningham, Henry S.: 58–59

Dalhousie, Earl (Marquess) of: 15

185